You Can't Make This Stuff Up
REALLY!

by Kenneth McClure *with* Charlotte Nelson

WESTBOW
PRESS®
A DIVISION OF THOMAS NELSON
& ZONDERVAN

WestBow Press books may be ordered through booksellers or by contacting:

WestBow Press
A Division of Thomas Nelson & Zondervan
1663 Liberty Drive
Bloomington, IN 47403
www.westbowpress.com
1 (866) 928-1240

Because of the dynamic nature of the Internet, any web addresses or
links contained in this book may have changed since publication and
may no longer be valid. The views expressed in this work are solely those
of the author and do not necessarily reflect the views of the publisher,
and the publisher hereby disclaims any responsibility for them.

Any people depicted in stock imagery provided by Getty Images are
models, and such images are being used for illustrative purposes only.
Certain stock imagery © Getty Images.

ISBN: 978-1-9736-6925-8 (sc)
ISBN: 978-1-9736-6926-5 (hc)
ISBN: 978-1-9736-6924-1 (e)

Library of Congress Control Number: 2019909688

Print information available on the last page.

WestBow Press rev. date: 11/25/2019

From our cradles, our mothers never stopped
encouraging us in our spiritual journey.
Our mates continued to play this role until they took
up residence in Heaven. We have been blessed!

Acknowledgments

– To all those who have died, recognized or unrecognized, who have made this book possible. Because of you, your relatives have bravely stepped in to plan your memorial service, thus bringing us to the elements of the ridiculous, sublime, and sometimes absurd.

– To our many funeral home friends who have shared the funnier side of an otherwise serious side of life.

– To our dear friend and PC Guru, Tim Morris, who kept one of us from throwing one PC (*not to mention one author!*) off the nearest bridge, and who found chapters which had mistakenly been lost in the middle of the night.

– To Willis Hamm, our talented artist whose wonderful sense of humor made him the perfect choice for illustrating some difficult chapters.

– To all our faithful and patient friends who kept asking us, "Is your book done yet?" or "Is it almost finished?"

– To our families who mostly refrained from asking those questions but were always willing to laugh with us when we shared some hilarious tidbit. (*At least we thought it was funny!*) Bless them!

– To Bob and Suzanne Hofmeister, our faithful prayer warriors who prayed for us and for the book to be published.

Disclaimer

YOU CAN'T MAKE THIS STUFF UP... REALLY! is a memoir, reflecting the authors' present recollections of events experienced during their years in ministry. All names, times, locations, events have been changed to protect both the living and the now dead, while not intending to play upon anyone's genuine grief.

Proper storytelling is a sophisticated art, with enhancement where characters tell their story, acting it out in real time, building suspense along with laughter. A simple story can be told dozens of times, each with that individual's recollection, but the end results are the same, laughter.

Although the subject matter within our book can be a sensitive matter, it is our goal to show the other side of human nature. One of the greatest tools in bringing healing is laughter, recalling special events in a life, and there is nothing funnier than laughing at oneself!

Contents

Glossary

- "Spanning the globe to bring you the constant variety of sports ... the thrill of victory... and the agony of defeat." This was ABC's opening narrative for "Wide World of Sports" 1961-1998. The thrill of understanding the "victory" of a word to the agony of "defeat" in not knowing its true meaning is why we have included a glossary.

- Shuga: affectionate name for a mate, southern way for "Sugar"

- purdy: pretty

- wake: also known as the "viewing", held the night before a funeral when friends and family can "view" the deceased

- "bless his heart:" phrase used before or after a derogatory remark about someone which makes it acceptable

- B Movie: low budget film in the 1940's and 1950's

- Georgia Peach: a pretty girl in Georgia

- Preach-ah: Southern pronunciation of "preacher"

- hard road: as opposed to a gravel road

- vapors: hot flashes

- cooties: slang word for head lice

- Terms used for "dying"

    passed
    passed on
    crossed over
    snuffed out the last cigar
    bought the farm
    check, please
    left this world

The following terms may be found in other books:

    bite the dust
    bite the big one
    cash in ones chips
    pushing up daisies
    go belly up
    give up the ghost
    kick the bucket

Introduction

If you have picked up this book and have read as far as the introduction, there is a strong possibility that your taste in humor is made for this book, or maybe you're just downright more curious than is good for you. Humor or comedy is a subjective choice because it depends on how we look at life and the experiences life has thrown our way. What is funny for one individual might be completely boring to another. But nothing is as funny as being able to laugh at one's self!

Ever found yourself in a situation where you wanted to laugh but couldn't? There was something in what you were experiencing that caused you to see the humorous side of life. The harder you tried not to laugh the more the impossibility of not was about to erupt. Your defense mechanism began by biting the inside of your mouth, advancing to the tip of your tongue to holding your handkerchief over your mouth. You tried everything in your power not to laugh but in the end your body began shaking, hitting close to a magnitude of a six point seven earthquake aftershock to those seated next to you. If that was your experience, YOU CAN'T MAKE THIS STUFF UP . . . REALLY! It's your kind of humor.

When the germination of this book began, I called my childhood friend, Charlotte, for her input, seeing she was a church organist and had played for many a funeral. Between the two of us, we shared over (*number of years – 60 for me*) causing us to believe we had heard it all, seen it all, and experienced it all. Although not all-encompassing, what you will find in this collection of true events is what we've experienced over the years. Within these pages, we meant nothing macabre or morbid, just dysfunction at its finest.

Some of it will cause a healthy belly laugh, or even require a moment to digest it before it hits you. It will either be subtle, dark, light, or challenging to your thought of it being completely over the top. Either way, it is meant to make you smile and laugh at human nature. Feel free to laugh out loud.

Each funeral we've been involved with has taught us that no two funerals are alike, but each is a new experience with the potential for the unheard of. The reason? Human nature hasn't basically changed since the beginning of time. There is no such thing as a "normal" funeral. Although there is a heavy side of grief in one, there is always a flip side of the same coin that can be observed at the present time or later when there is ample time to reflect, leaving the head shaking while thinking, YOU CAN'T MAKE THIS STUFF UP.

It has been said, "Never discount anything in your past for it can still be used in incredible ways." King Solomon reminded us that laughter is good medicine, as well as, "There is a time to weep, and a time to laugh, a time to mourn, and a time to dance." Simply said, if we don't laugh, we'll cry, and laughter can help us get through some of the more difficult times of our lives.

There is nothing funny about death nor is it our intent to make light of it. We've all walked through that lonely valley personally, or experienced it with a friend. In the process, we often become aware there were some absurd and funny moments and characters, along with dialog and mannerisms that brought a smile to our faces and minds that helped in finding closure.

Within each story, all names, locations, and times have been deliberately altered to protect the identity of those involved, both living and now deceased. If some of these situations appear to be your own, it is because many people have experienced similar reactions. Remember, nothing is as funny as being able to laugh at one's self!

What Did You Say Your Name Was?

It has been my long-standing nightmare (*Yes, I sometimes HAVE nightmares and don't always GIVE them!*) that I would somehow get into the wrong funeral. What would I do? Do I go along with the mix-up and lie? Well, it never hurts to come prepared for such an event, should it happen, God forbid! I reasoned that I could say, (*with crossed fingers behind my back*), "He was such a good friend. We're surely going to miss him. You have our deepest sympathies," while trying to fade in among the baskets of flowers in the room and heading for the nearest exit. I've always thought it wise to nod at the other guests, hoping no one will speak to me. If stopped while leaving, I have contemplated placing a handkerchief over my mouth to feign grief and therefore have an inability to speak. I could shake my head slightly from side to side, giving the appearance of being torn up with grief. This should give enough time to clear the room. Nine times out of ten, people not wanting to get involved will give someone a free pass out of the room. I realized I probably shouldn't stop and pick up a book of funeral home matches on my way out. Poor taste!

Unfortunately, my recurring nightmare became reality some years ago. It all began when I wanted to show off my new beautiful bride. Kathy and I hadn't been married more than a couple of months, and I was still in the "show and tell" mode as I demonstrated to any resident Yankees what a true Southern Belle was like, for I had found me a delicious Georgia Peach. Of course she's my new bride. I've never heard anyone say, "I'd like you to meet my old bride," and lived long enough to tell it!

Our little road trip with my new bride began with explaining why this particular road trip included a funeral home visit. I shared with her that several years earlier I had just finished getting my master's degree and had accepted a summer position in a small mid-west town. That summer experience turned into a full time position that lasted for a number of years. I expressed to her that it turned out to be one of those wonderful chapters in my life that I wouldn't trade for a million bucks. It was rich with experiences and great people, some who remain close friends even after all these years, and who know my "elevator of humor" doesn't always go all the way to the top. (*She'd already figured that one out!*) Having grown up in a large mid-west city, I wasn't quite ready to move into a small town that was limited in numbers but did include a large farming community. Our town consisted of approximately 5000 people, give or take a few. Another 500 could be added if the farmers were counted.

I'll tell you how small (*could I say INFINITESIMAL?*) the town was. It had a grain elevator, a drug store, hardware and grocery store, one drive-in eatery, and a courthouse square. Oh, I forgot, a Chevrolet dealership connected to the gas station and the John Deere Tractor dealership. It had three funeral homes. It seemed to me that not that many people were dying to support three but one was for the Catholics, one for the more affluent people, and then there was Mr. M.'s funeral home for all the other folks, the "salt of the earth" type.

Mr. M. attended the church where I was employed as youth director. My hours were flexible, which gave me some free time to help Mr. M. at the funeral home, with the elders' permission, of course. His older son had passed away and the younger one wanted nothing to do with the funeral business. Mr. M. was in need of help, and since I always wanted to drive one of those big old hearses, and it was extra money for me, I jumped at the chance. I guess I've just had this secret thing about nice, long, big black Cadillac hearses. Gotta love those classic lines and of course, their shining black finish.

A lot of the incidents that appear in this book came from those years I helped Mr. M. This gave me a whole new perspective of the funeral business as well as human nature. Our relationship was like a lovable old grandfather and his grandson. We hit it off right away. Having him in my life was like therapy to me as I had lost my Paw-Paw, my hero, only a few months before. Mr. M. soon filled in the emptiness in my life, not replacing Paw-Paw, but helping me over those difficult days. Our relationship was so strong that he offered me the funeral home, "lock-stock-and-barrel." All I would have had to do was attend embalming school for six months. I graciously declined, knowing that this wasn't my permanent calling. Besides, a big hearse loses some of its luster after awhile, especially when it turned out to be a light baby blue one, with a red dome bubble light on top! (*It wasn't even a Cadillac!*)

Mr. M. had reached those years when he had contributed his share to society and was well past retirement age. He had been coroner and medical examiner for years. But one thing for sure, Mr. and Mrs. M. were loved by the people. If someone didn't have the money to bury a loved one, Mr. M. would work something out. Payback might be in fresh vegetables in the summer, yard work, or even a few simple repair jobs around the place. But no matter the financial condition of the clientele, he turned no one away, even if it meant a dollar down and a dollar a week payback. Mr. M. and Myrtle lived above the funeral home, and many a night during the summer they would invite me to eat supper with them. I could always tell that what we had to eat had a direct correlation to what somebody was paying back. If there happened to be meat in among the fresh vegetables that meant someone had given Mr. M. some money on his bill. Veggies only meant no money had been collected. Those were some good times around that old kitchen table with its bright flowery oilcloth table covering.

My bride and I pulled up in front of the funeral home, and right away she slid closer to me than ever before. (*This was before seat belt laws.*) She was almost under the steering wheel. She immediately grabbed my arm and said, "Are you sure we want to go in there?" Looking at the parking lot and all of the vehicles that were there, she continued, "What are you going to say? You probably don't even know these people, just Mr. M. and his wife!"

Being a newly ordained groom, I could see my chest swelling as I said in braggadocio tones, "Don't worry, sweetheart. This is a piece of cake. I know what to say and I'll protect you. I've done this hundreds of times!" I knew that now was the time to show off one of my many people skills on how to say the right thing at the right time.

Looking down into her face, I could tell that she wasn't buying a bit of it. (*Her facial expression could be related to the look a man gets when he refuses to stop and ask directions when lost.*) I blocked out immediately what I saw in those blue eyes, knowing that the odds of them saying, "I told you so," were a hundred to one! If only I had listened to what the Talmud had to say! "No matter how short your wife is, lean down and take her advice."

But alas, with my "husband masculinity" on the line, I had to show no fear as I quickly replied, "Nah! Just act like you know these people, smile and just be your sweet self."

"But there's a funeral going on," she said, with doubt in her voice, hoping I would change my mind about going in.

"It's just a visitation," I tried to explain with assuring words. "If it were a funeral, you would see the cars lined up behind the hearse. It'll be fine! Just trust me."

Little did I know that I was about to eat those words, and without salt or pepper to improve their taste. That day I would learn that when that powerful 4' 11" package of southern charm spoke, I best listen. Oh, the hard lessons we prideful men could avoid if only we would listen to our wives. They have such wonderful insight at times that we fail to take heed of! Hopefully, I would remember my do's and don'ts and this funeral home visit would go as planned.

Stepping out of the car I was suddenly made aware of the disarray and deterioration of the funeral home. The two-story building was in need of much repair, but a simple coat of paint would have been good for starters. It reminded me of something out of some B horror movie, lacking only a few black crows and numerous lightning bolts bouncing around. Add the scary pipe organ followed by several bats flying overhead and we could have an Edgar Allan Poe backdrop! I must admit it was nothing like what I had left years before. I just knew that if Sherman had marched through this small farming town and observed that run-down structure, he would have struck a match to the place and rightly so!

Glancing around the parking lot I knew this was a low budget funeral, better known in the funeral industry as "low budget show!" No disrespect in mind, it just means that not a lot of money had been spent on this funeral; however, no expense was spared with their monster trucks and souped-up cars. My observation was further confirmed by the dress of the clientele.

The crowd of people in the front yard and on the front porch of the funeral home was a polite bunch of "good old boys," dressed in their blue jeans, cowboy hats and boots. Not only was their conversation "colorful", but it was accented with smoking, chewing, and spitting. Nodding and smiling, we made our way through the crowd. Hats were removed, followed by nods and smiles, possibly all because of the way we were dressed. I quickly whispered in my wife's ear, "Don't you dare wave your Queen Elizabeth wave. Just smile and nod!"

The front door of the funeral home opened for us, introducing the latest employee, a distant relative of Egor. He was an elderly gentleman, I would guess in his late 70s, wearing what appeared to be a slept-in-pin-striped suit covering his five by five body. He wore a brightly-patterned Hawaiian shirt under his suit coat, the kind you see in stores and wonder who in their right mind would buy a shirt like that. (*Maybe to make people think you've been to Hawaii?*) He had no neck, only a round bald head resting on his shoulders, with a stringy little ponytail trying to make up for his lack of hair. To be perfectly honest, bless his heart, he looked like something one feeds peanuts to on a visit to the zoo!

His glasses were covered in finger prints, raising my suspicions that they hadn't been cleaned in years. The only thing lacking would have been a large pink diaper pin holding the glass to the frame on one side. I felt a tug on my arm pulling me over so my ear could become the recipient of my wife's admonition, "Stop! You're staring!"

We had no more entered the room when I happened to look toward the open casket, hearing a young lady yell out, "You came!" Rushing toward me was this tall, slender woman, the crowd parting as she made her way toward my wife and myself. In the time it took for me to brace myself, every neuron in my brain was trying to fire but to no avail! "Who is this woman? I can't remember! I don't recognize her at all! WHAT DO I SAY?"

I quickly looked at my wife who gave me that smug look that I had already learned to realize meant, "I told you so!" Only this time there was added across her smile, "Let's see you get out of this one, smarty!" Looks to me like God gave women simply to keep their husbands in check.

All I could think was, don't let this clueless facial expression be obvious, because the fast-approaching Mack Truck was headed my way. Not only would I have the impact of being hit broadside by this 18-Wheeler, but a machine gun speech pattern would dazzle my comprehension. Her rapid firing speech sucked every ounce of air out of my lungs as I tried to interrupt her, but with no luck. I wanted to yell at her at some time or another, "Breathe!" But that would have had no effect on her as she appeared to be one who didn't need air to survive.

Before I could brace myself for the head on collision with this disaster waiting to happen, she threw her arms around my neck and said for the whole world to hear, "I knew you would come

. . . I just knew it!" Running out of air again from being squeezed so hard, I started slowly and gently peeling her off my being and proceeded to introduce her to my bride. But STOP!

What's this lady's name? Who do I introduce to my bride? Before I had a chance to worry about that, utter an instant prayer, or yell for help from anyone present, she said, "Come!" with the zeal of one showing off her new car. "You've got to see Daddy. He looks so natural, just like he was asleep." Not walking, but dragging me through the crowd, she ushered Kathy and me up to the casket. "Daddy thought so much of you," she said again. "You're all he talked about! Doesn't he look so good? The hole in the side of his head doesn't really show. You think so? Wax! Got a good price on the casket! Like the color? Matches his suit, don't you think? Oh," pulling on a man's arm who had been standing behind us, "I want you to meet my husband, Rocky!"

There he stood this tall, unshaven, lanky, skinny specimen in his tank-top, bandanna headband and leather wristbands. "He's a drummer," she loudly proclaimed. "He's with the Bumper Stickers heavy metal rock band." Rocky, who appeared to be living in another world with his apparently fried brain and definite hearing loss, stood beating the air with his imaginary drum sticks as she introduced him, without a last name.

Firing off more brain neurons, I prayed, "Dear God, I promise you anything, just get me out of this mess and tell me who this woman is!" When my prayer got a busy signal, I could just imagine God sitting in heaven, laughing His head off watching me squirm trying to get out of what I had stepped in. Not hearing from heaven when I prayed, I quickly turned to my wife, hoping to be rescued. Her facial expression offered no advice either, telling me I was still in deep water. I had better learn to swim or it was all going down.

At the head of this casket was a large oval floral arrangement in the shape of a clock with the hands stopped on the time the deceased had died. I quickly looked for a card with a name or some clue attached to it like, "To the (*Blank*) Family, with deepest sympathy! The such-n-such family" Great! Nothing! I would have settled for it had it said, "Jesus called and he answered!" Maybe then Jesus might have given me a hint as to the deceased's last name.

When I looked down into the casket, with my wife hanging on to one arm cutting off the blood circulation, and this other woman, (*whoever she was*) hanging on to the other, I knew I couldn't drop to my knees and pray for the rapture to happen. The best I could hope for was a lack of blood flow that would cause me to faint, taking me out of this situation.

To my amazement, the deceased had his right hand resting on a dial telephone and his left hand on a small calculator. Over his right shoulder lay a large yellow legal pad and pen and a daily planner rested on his left shoulder.

"Isn't that just like Daddy," the woman said, patting the various items in the casket. "Daddy worked for a large tomato catsup company where he supervised the field crews. Daddy," she said, "wasn't ever more than a few feet from the phone, calculator, and his legal pad." As she kept talking, my creative brain neurons started firing one more time. Wouldn't it be funny to hook up that phone in the deceased's hand and have it go off during the funeral service? Suddenly I was brought back to reality by the gentle pull on my right arm from my bride, allowing "this woman", whoever she was, to continue her talk about my relationship with her father and how much he liked working with me.

In case you're wondering what I said to this unidentified woman . . . none of the "no no's" (*listed in another chapter*). I simply grunted, smiled as she made all of her remarks, even played the blushing card of false humility at the compliments she was extending. Basically I just let her vent her grief as I realized that it wasn't about me, but it was all about her and her dealing with her loss. If she thought she knew me and it helped with her coping, then it was worth it all. I could have said a lot of things at the moment, exposing the whole charade and it might have embarrassed her in thinking she knew me, but I learned something that day. "Don't take my grief away from me," meaning, we let people mourn in their own way and time. My closing remark was, "I can tell you were very fond of your father. You're in our thoughts and prayers!"

Quickly we headed for the door, and passing the guest book,

my bride said with a chuckle in her voice, "Aren't you going to sign the guest register?" to which I quickly responded, "And have her just as confused as we were when she later reads the names and wonders who we were? I don't think so! Let's go!" So much for "show-and-tell" of my new bride!

The short walk down the hall, past the office and up the backstairs to Mr. M.'s living quarters was extremely quiet between the two of us. Halfway up the stairs I looked into my wife's eyes, where I saw the words, clearer than a neon billboard flashing, "I told you so," as she smiled graciously without saying a word. It was followed by a squeeze on the arm and the look that only a genteel southern lady could communicate without saying a single word, "I love you!"

I Do Get Hazard Pay, Don't I?

What do antebellum homes and "Have Black Suit, Will Travel" have in common? As the proverbial saying goes, "I'm glad you asked!" Place an antebellum home with a wraparound porch, anywhere in the nation, and nine times out of ten you have located the local funeral home.

And the "black suit?" Most funeral directors have a reverend or two on call who own a black suit and can be depended upon in case the deceased's family has no religious connection. Thus the standing joke, "Have black suit, will travel," has been attached to ministers.

One morning, feeling in a particularly jovial mood (*and knowing the caller, thanks to Caller ID*), I answered the phone with, "Have black suit, will travel" After a brief laugh, details, times, etc. were given, my services were once again required. Although the family in need was not affiliated with my particular denomination, I always approached the opportunity to minister to a family in their time of grief as an opportunity to serve my fellow man.

Arriving at the funeral home for the visitation, I felt honored to find there was a single parking space left in front of the home. *(How could I not think it was left just for me?)* But as I looked toward the front porch of this large antebellum-style building, I noticed that there was a dense blue haze surrounding the group of individuals gathered on the wraparound porch of this stately mansion. As I stepped out of my car, my attention also turned to a fast-approaching fire truck, flashing lights and all. Was the funeral home on fire and my services weren't needed? Already I was beginning to wonder what was just around the corner for this pastor!

As I approached the front door, those on the steps and front porch seemed to part, making way for me to walk among them, causing me to feel like Moses parting the Red Sea once again, only on a smaller scale. I nodded a gracious "thank you" as a member of the cloth would be required to do. My bubble was quickly popped when I realized all that "parting of the way" wasn't because I was some important dignitary. Instead, I was just a simple reverend with the sign of the fish on the back of my car... but dressed in a manner totally foreign to them. I realized that my suit and tie were no longer accepted funeral attire. Obviously, I thought to myself, the majority had not received the office memo for the occasion.

I was greeted at the door by my funeral home director friend who, upon shaking my hand, rolled his eyes almost to the back of his head as he displayed facial expressions that read loud and clear, "You're not gonna believe this!"

I was instantly led into Slumber Room #1, whereupon further observation; it almost seemed that I was being led into a tattoo and body piercing parlor rather than a visitation room. I realized it was one of those moments where "Old School" meets "New School"! Where "Old School" doesn't want to move but society is dragging it screaming and yelling into their century.

There was a strange aroma floating through the air matching that on the front porch, but not even close to resembling the traditional funeral home fragrance of flowers, past and present.

Condolences were exchanged with the immediate family as we approached the open casket. Located with the deceased were football memorabilia, not just a few pieces but enough to stock a tailgate party! To further amaze me, I beheld packages of chewing gum, which had been placed under the arms, hands, and around the head of the deceased. Not a variety of chewing gum, but one brand in particular. I have observed over the years that it is not uncommon for items near and dear to the deceased to be placed in the casket.

Suddenly, I found myself thrust into the presence of the "grieving" widow. I had been warned that she and the deceased were in the final stages of a nasty divorce, and none of the family liked her or wanted her there, so I was to be prepared for anything. But prepared for anything, I wasn't! Before I could utter, "I'm so deeply sorry for your loss," or "You have my deepest sympathy," out of nowhere, I was tapped on the shoulder only to turn and meet the deceased's current girlfriend.

The air in the room suddenly became filled with the potential explosion as these two forces met.

Flanked next to "waiting to break my ankles" if I chose sides, stood what appeared to be the girlfriend's bodyguards. "Do I run, faint, pray?" I asked myself. Regardless, here stood two unsightly giants of human flesh sporting gold-capped teeth and appearing to have come out of some action movie.

Both of these giants had shaved heads and wore dog collars covered in spikes minus the dog leash. Each of their ears had six or seven piercings. Both of their shirts were open revealing rippling muscles as they stood with their large ham hock arms folded across their chests as if to say, "We dare you to make a move, runt!" They had nothing to fear since I wouldn't even shake their hands! Hey, I'm not a runt! I'm nearly six feet tall the last I checked! Nevertheless, if I got a spurt of bravery and did start to "mess" with them, I knew I would soon become a grease spot on the carpet even before I was able to go down to the casket room and pick out my own box.

So here I stood, flanked with the girlfriend on one side whose dress left very little to the imagination, covered in tattoos from top to bottom, and the ex-wife dressed like a member of an "All-Saints Day" celebration. But credit must be given to the girlfriend; her arms' and legs' tattoos matched her neck ones. Gotta love a woman who coordinates her ensemble!

Approaching the possible battlefield (*and giving me a second or two reprieves*) was a young lady carrying a large tray hung around her neck filled with chewing gum. She had been circling the room like a cigarette girl in an old black and white B movie. "Gum?" she asked as if offering me a pot of gold.

"No, thank you," I replied. If I was about to be tackled by the two commandos, the last thing I wanted was a wad of gum in my mouth, causing my instantaneous death by choking or, at the least, the inability to cry out for help. Even if I weren't the object of the pending attack, I wasn't taking any chances!

Suddenly, my soon to be a knight in shining armor, dressed as the funeral director, took me by the arm and quickly ushered me into his office. The movement was so fast that I couldn't help but make sure he didn't have a tape measure in his hand, (*They're always sizing you up for future business!*) I took a seat where we struck up what appeared to be a normal conversation.

To my surprise, he commented on the attending guests at the visitation and that he thought he had seen it all in his twenty years in this business, but this beat all! Finally, his conversation got around to the two large brown paper bags located behind the casket in the visitation room with items to be placed in the casket before it was finally closed. Already there were cartons of cigarettes, lighters, six-packs of beer, beef jerky, a Lotto ticket, cheese crackers, nuts, gum, (*of course*) and various kinds of candy.

"Where else can this fiasco be going?" I asked. His reply was short and quick, "Just be prepared for anything, trust me!"

On the day of the funeral, I was awakened by one of the loudest claps of thunder I believe I had ever heard, enough to knock me clear out of bed and wake the dead at the same time, no pun intended! Could this be a foreshadowing of things to come today?

I found my answering machine was blinking with a message from the funeral director that the fifth request for changes in the order of service in the last two days had just come in. These request changes are not so unusual when you have all the relatives nearby who must have a part in the arrangements. They all know somebody who will do such-and-such in the service, making it "right purdy!" Thank goodness Aunt Susie had passed on or she would have insisted that she sang "Ave Maria" in her wobbling 89-year-old nasal-soprano voice.

The final requests were for an open casket during the service, a Jericho March, and I could give my little "ditty" then. I was also not to forget the two large brown paper sacks behind the casket that had more items to be placed in and around the deceased.

Pushing the off button on the answering machine, I had to chuckle to myself, "a little ditty?" In reality, I think I need another cup of coffee and a couple of aspirins. . . .Oh, yes . . . no fist pounding today, but there WILL be talking about making those final reservations for the afterlife!

Several hours later, arriving at the funeral home, I immediately went straight to the main office to see if there were any new changes since I had left home. You guessed it. New changes waited.

For starters, a gentle reminder was given to make sure that all the items in the brown paper bags had been placed in the casket. I also was to check and see that the deceased's dress shoes had been removed and his favorite tennis shoes put on his feet. I thought that was the undertaker's job. O well, whatever!

Next, I tried to explain that a Celtic singer had been added and would be singing a cappella, a word which obviously hadn't crossed the path of this 80+ part-time funeral home employee. Ever tried to enunciate to this aging (*bless his heart!*) undertaker who belonged downstairs in a box of his own (his choice of color and style, of course) how to pronounce "a cappella". We went through Acapulco, Acka poo poo, and other sounding ways I won't print, when finally he said, "I can't say it, let alone know what it means!"

"Tell you what," I responded."She'll be sanging it without a (*and with a veeeery long, drawn out twang*), pie-an-o." That he got!

Watching the clock and seeing the hour of the service drawing nearer, I sauntered down the hallway and observed the current girlfriend walking back and forth, crying, and very upset. Every time someone would walk up to her to offer comfort, she would shake her head "no". As I approached her she politely said, "I'm fine." At that point I was ushered by a younger undertaker into the visitation room for a final prayer with the family before the service, but not without first noticing once again, the "cigarette-style girl" with her tray passing out gum. This time people were taking whole packages of gum instead of single sticks as some had done before.

As others gathered around the casket, I noticed the "ex-soon-to-be-was-is-wife-widow???" Talk about confusion! It was fast becoming the famous baseball skit, "Who's on First?" As she walked toward the casket, the crowd of mourners quickly stepped aside as if she was crying out in Biblical times, "Unclean, unclean. Leprosy!"

There she stood in her "All Saints Day" attire, sobbing up a storm. Yet no one moved toward her to comfort her. She stood alone in enemy territory. Slowly she placed her hands on top of her deceased husband's hands and began talking to him. From what I could see, she currently, or had in the past, loved him dearly, enough to enter the lions' den to say her last good-byes. She was one brave woman!

Slowly the ex turned and walked out of the room, taking her seat by herself in the back of the chapel. But her empty place in front of the casket was quickly replaced by the current girlfriend. With one determined move of reclaiming her territorial rights, she flung herself across the deceased, putting Lady Macbeth or any drama queen to shame with her daring performance.

She stood, dry-eyed, surveyed the crowd and seeing she had everyone's attention, turned on the fake tears and flung herself down across the deceased for a repeat performance. By this time the visitation room doors were closed and guests were asked to move to the chapel. Those remaining were supposed to be just the immediate family, which appeared to have grown overnight. One by one as they filed by the casket for the final time, family members and friends placed packets of gum in the casket. Exchanging glances with the funeral director, we both shared a baffled look as to why this strange activity was taking place. Was it some wild tribal ritual, a secret cult minus a special handshake? Shrugging my shoulders, I said to him, "If I knew the answer, I'm sure I would be a candidate for the Nobel Peace Prize or some such prestigious award!"

Through the years of my experiences, I've noticed that something super dramatic happens when the director opens the double doors of the funeral chapel, steps into the room, and announces to the audience, "All rise." It has always reminded me of what the Sergeant-at-Arms proclaims prior to the State of the Union addresses. It does lack a bit of presidential luster and pomp, although what could one really expect when it's a funeral? Drawing a large breath for assurance, knowing I had gone through my checklist twice making sure my shirt was tucked, tie was straight, it was time to make the "plunge", ready or not. I made my entrance, walking straight to the platform, remembering that the eight pallbearers were behind me, and I had to keep my composure, not knowing whether to cry, laugh, or run.

I had been informed ahead of time that all eight pallbearers had been instructed as to what the attire of the day was to be, suits and ties, or a nice dress shirt with a tie. I hated the thought of telling my informant his instructions had fallen on deaf ears.

Making their grand entrance was this gang of eight, pallbearers from all parts of the country. Archie, up here from Joe's Catfish Shack in Carroll Country, took it on himself to be the official lead pallbearer, figured his clean "Wife Beater" T-shirt gave him the authority he needed. He did have the common sense not to wear the beer T-shirt he had gotten free from the Johnny Lube. Following next were several of the "good old boys" wearing free T-shirts advertising the local stock car races, Beer Jamboree, etc. all led by Cousin Harold, his next-door neighbor Clettis Joe, and then the whole Fire Station number 9 dart team, which completed the eight-plus various and sundry "honorary" pallbearers.

Upon reaching the platform, my eyes beheld this gang of eight in their "formal attire" now seated in the front row of the chapel. I nearly yelled, "Someone call 911!" Instead, I silently prayed, "Dear God, please let whatever that is bulging below their lower lips and in their cheeks be gum and not what I think it is!" It wasn't gum. This explained the presence of the Dixie cups in their hands and the "not so discreet" necessity of relieving the accumulated spit.

The first to give the eulogy came bouncing down the center aisle from the very back of the chapel. (*You would think any speaker would want to sit as close to the front as possible. Not this one!*) It was "Old Home Week at the Mortuary" as she high fived the mourners seated next to the aisle, her ponytails bouncing in the breeze, one on each side sticking out like horns.

When this woman stepped up on the platform, I stood to show respect for all womanhood (*as I had been taught*). Much to my surprise, "What's-His-Name guest speaker (*was he on the printed program??*) now seated to my right looking important, dressed in his suit and tie, remained seated until I motioned with my hand and said in a low whisper, "Stand up!"

He finally stood, stuttering, "Oh...oh...yes." They just don't make professionals like they used to! My mother up in heaven, bless her heart, would be abhorred had I not stood at the appropriate time. But then Mother might also have been abhorred by the appearance of this current speaker. She was wearing a long moo-moo-type dress and black untied high-top tennis shoes, giving her the look of a twenty-something "Granny Grunt". Paris runways look out! Nevertheless, she spread out her papers on the pulpit and I thought, "We'll be here till midnight!"

By this time I had taken my seat and had left "What's-His-Name" standing by the "fashion statement". "Psst", I said discreetly, "you can sit down now," gesturing toward his seat. I was secretly afraid he might wander off, looking for a place to sit while surfing the audience.

Standing within eighteen inches of my face came the spicy language (*deleted here!*) exploding from this young lady. "We're here to celebrate the good old times we had while our friend was alive, and they were some good old times, too!" I instantly had come to the conclusion that I would pray for the rapture to occur before any other disaster could erupt. But...it wasn't to be.

Mentally picking myself up off the floor and in spite of the language, the service continued with the next lady on the program singing a drinking song followed by a poem she had written for the occasion. She had requested to be placed at the beginning of the service since, as she explained, "I've got another gig to sing at".

She was quickly followed by "What's-His-Name." He started out by saying, "I have a photographic memory, (*repeating it several times in the service*) I remember it all!" His entire speech was about himself and not a single word was spoken about the deceased or the family in their time of grief. Later I would learn that he and the deceased had been cellmates at one time.

Looking at the order of service, it appeared that the remaining time was mine and now it had the potential of running much more smoothly, I thought! Standing to read the obituary I soon learned the true meaning of "Don't count your chickens before they hatch!"

I was only a few seconds into the obituary when two ladies in the front row began to signal me. At first, it began with small gestures toward a nearby lady and grew to movements which reminded me of airport personnel directing a Jumbo 747 approaching the gate. I tried to ignore the finger pointing and waving but finally, I had no choice but to stop and ask what the problem was. I asked myself if I had done something wrong, or maybe something inappropriate. Millions of questions shot through my mind before I regained my composure and asked, "Yes? Is there something you wish to tell me?"

Slowly one of the ladies in the front row leaned forward; looking both directions as if crossing a busy street, she puckered her lips and whispered something. "I beg your pardon?" I said. She then nodded her head in quick upward and sideways movements, her eyes following her head motions toward someone who was seated beside her. But still, nothing registered.

Standing there with a dumb look on my face, I was still trying to understand what was so important that this funeral had to be interrupted. I remembered we had gone over the obituary with the family prior to the service to verify that no one had been left out. So what might it be?

Leaning even further out of her seat, in great danger of leaving it in favor of the floor, she repeated her mannerisms, this time talking in a louder whisper, "Aunt Stella".

For whatever reason, I couldn't help but repeat what I had just heard. "Aunt Stella, who?" Instantly it was like all the air in the room had been sucked out and a unison gasp was heard from the family members. It was a wonder they didn't qualify for a group whiplash discount at the local hospital as all eyes turned to Aunt Stella. (*For the record, the name Aunt Stella is a made up name because I just like the way it sounds. But in my defense of my Aunt Stella, almost every living family has an Aunt Stella whether or not they want to admit it.*)

One look told me I had overlooked the matriarch, the Queen Bee of the clan. There she sat, her arms crossed as if waiting for someone to cross her. (*If looks could kill, at least I was in the right place!*) Aunt Stella was dressed for the occasion! Her hair was piled on top of her head fulfilling "the taller the hair, the closer to God" slogan; she wore cat-eyed glasses covered with rhinestones and sequins and had enough face powder to qualify her as being dead. Her bright red lipstick covered not only her mouth but the surrounding areas as well. She was so puffed up about herself that there could be no doubt that she ruled the roost, and how dare I, a lowly, simple preacher, forget her name and her rank (*I'm sure she had a serial number as well!*) in this clan!

Her name had been omitted from the obituary since everyone assumed it wouldn't matter because she wouldn't show up anyway! Wrong! It did and she did! Funerals were just not her thing, normally not large enough audiences for her grand entrances. Regardless, I was sure it would be "you know what" to pay when the service was over.

I needed to make it very clear that the mistake was not mine and to please accept my sincere apologies on behalf of the family.

My heartbeat was slowly coming back to a somewhat normal rate as I asked the forgiveness of dear Aunt Stella and proceeded with the message.

I was no more than five minutes into the message and everything was flowing along smoothly. I had read more family-requested Scripture, prayed, and was now getting to the meat of what God had placed on my heart. I had just finished reading John 3:16, "For God so loved the world that He gave his only begotten Son, that whosoever believeth in Him should not perish, but has everlasting life."

As I paused to let the meaning of the verse sink in, the silence was suddenly shattered by the ringing of a cell phone coming from the vicinity of the family. The obnoxious ringtone's intrusion was a German polka band playing, "When the Saints Go Marching In". Well, at least the song was appropriate for a funeral! The tuba's "om pa pas" was relentless as the search for the cell phone continued.

"Hold that thought, Preach-ah, gotta take this call. It'll only take a moment! It's gotta be somebody important! You know what I mean?" Who could possibly be this rude? You guessed it! Aunt Stella, the Queen Bee herself!

Daring to crawl into the cave with this old mother bear, I threw caution to the wind and said, "Excuse me, Miss Stella, but would you be so kind as to (*I wanted to say 'remove yourself' but I didn't!*) take that call in the other room? I'm sure it's important to you but that way we can get on with what we're trying to achieve!" I may as well have been talking to the deceased!

Pulling her oversized bag up off the floor, referring to it as her "purse", she began her panicked quest to find her ringing cell phone. "Here, hold this!" she said, handing items from her bag to those around her. After a few seconds of frantic searching, it was obvious she wasn't talking to Jesus by what she was saying under her breath. "It's okay, Preach-ah, I'll find it; it'll only take a minute. Then you can pick up where you left off!"

Later I was to learn that Aunt Stella was one of a kind. She had been born in the middle west but told everyone (*after seeing GONE*

WITH THE WIND eight times) that she was a gen-u-ine Southern Belle, born in the deep south, way below the Mason-Dixon Line. She was always trying to convince people that she was a true southerner by her thick, fake southern accent. People knew she was a Belle, but that her clapper was missing. When asked one day if she knew where the Line was, she replied, in her heaviest southern accent, " My goodness, of course, I do, Shuga! Everyone knows it's the line that goes around the center of the earth; it's called the equator!" In accord with true southern social dictates, no one ever told her differently.

Finding her phone (*thankfully!*), she flipped it open and as expected, answered in shades of Scarlett O'Hara. I was hoping that any moment she would yell, "I'll think about this tomorrow", but instead she disappointed me with a simple "Hello!" Then,"Edna? Well, what's up, Shuga?" Placing her hand over the mouthpiece and looking around the room at those who were staring at her, making sure she had an adequate audience, she continued in her syrupy fake Southern voice, "It's Edna. She's my dearest friend this week!"

She began fanning herself, flirting with her audience from behind the fan, which had appeared out of nowhere, and continued with Edna, proclaiming, "Why fiddle-de-dee, child, what could be your problem, especially interrupting such a glorious funeral service as this! I'm sorry you couldn't be here, you're really missing out!" Hearing only one side of the conversation, it wasn't too difficult to make out what was being said next on the other end of the line.

"I guess as good as he can, him bein' dead and all."

"You got the vapors again?"

"I knew it, I knew it! You've got those emotional flashes again!"

"Whatever gave you that idea? I'm appalled that you would think such a thing!" Fanning herself even faster, "Now I'm startin' to get the vapors!"

"PLEASE don't start cryin' or you'll have me cryin' and I've got to save my tears for later in the service."

"Excuse me, Miss Stella", I said, pointing to my watch. "We

need to get on with the service." Nothing I could do or say would faze her.

As I slowly retreated to my chair on the platform, I figured I was doomed and I better just let this thing play out and hopefully, in the end, I would win the game. Her one-sided conversation continued:

"Edna, just go down to the Piggly Wiggly and get yourself a frozen Mrs. Pete's pie, for heaven's sake!

"Really?"

"Well, you KNOW she didn't like your pie if she didn't have to re-apply her lipstick after she ate her third piece!"

Then, with a quick "Bye, Shuga", she was finished and she flipped her phone closed, turned around in her seat, and said in a commanding voice, "Pass my things back here to me, and you better not have taken anything either, ya hear?" Stuffing her things back into her "purse", she looked up at me and said, as if nothing had happened, "Carry on, Preach-ah, I'm done." With that, she folded her arms once again and sat back in her pew!

Not only was Aunt Stella done, so was I. There was no way I could recapture the sanity or the sanctity which had once prevailed. I quickly summarized and concluded the service, and as requested by the family, began the Jericho March.

Family members were quickly ushered out to the waiting limo as I waited to escort the casket out to the hearse. The funeral director quickly closed the casket and we started to leave the chapel when suddenly this strange sound started coming from within the casket. Someone had set the deceased's alarm on his watch to go off. Instantly, the funeral director started to lift the lid of the casket but I quickly put an end to that. I had had it. I had a headache, and we were going on with this service. Through clenched teeth, I said, "Don't you dare!"

Arriving at the cemetery and observing a fast-approaching thunderstorm, we climbed the steep rolling hills, and I immediately understood why the funeral home was pleased to have eight pallbearers rather than the standard six. Not only was it a very old graveyard, dating back to the turn of the century, but it was full of old trees with roots growing above ground making it necessary to watch every step I took.

Slowly the guests and I made our way to the open grave. There we stood under two tents with metal poles and a multitude of trees with the lightning getting ever so close. The funeral director whispered in my ear, "You better cut this short or we're in trouble," as the thunder increased its volume.

Don't ever tell me that our God in Heaven doesn't have a sense of humor or that He doesn't like to choreograph events in our lives, even during some of our saddest moments. I had just finished reading the Scripture when the director's eye telegraphed a panicked message: "Better hurry up! It's a-comin'!" I started to say, "And on that great resurrection morn, when the trumpet of the Lord shall sound. . ." when at that exact moment a colossal clap of thunder exploded, shaking the ground around us, thinking to myself, "Well, he got there!"

Quickly I said, "Let us pray!" I prayed a very short prayer and said, "This concludes our service."

Standing next to me was one of the deceased's buddies and I couldn't wait any longer to satisfy my curiosity. Quietly I asked, "Why the gum throughout this entire funeral?" He proceeded to tell me that he and all his buddies had grown up together, attended high school together, and were the best of friends. The trick among them was to sneak up from behind and slap a wad of chewed gum either into the person's hair or beard. "So that explains why the deceased had shaved his head," I responded, now with some clarity.

I started to make my way toward the family to express my sincere sympathy and assure them that I would be praying for them, when suddenly I added the grand finale, the exclamation point, to this entire funeral. I had been extremely careful, watching out for every overgrown root from the various trees, but failed to pay attention to one important item. Around the open grave, boards had been placed to hold the casket/vault lift. They were discreetly covered with artificial grass but my toe caught the corner of the boards. I started to fall face first into the open grave! It was the first time I was thankful to be wearing a suit on a very hot day because the director was able to grab my coattail as I was falling forward and saved me from making a complete fool of myself (*Would anyone even notice?*) and landing squarely on top of the casket!

Having regained my composure as I now stood upright, I straightened my tie, adjusted my coat, and made my way down the row of chairs. Thankfully, my beet-red face could be blamed on the heat and not my near miss dive into the grave! My "Hallmark Moment"? Not even close! Rather, YOU CAN'T MAKE THIS STUFF UP...REALLY!

All in a Day's Work

I've often been asked, if I had to do it all over, knowing what I know now, would I choose the ministry and church work again? Without a moment of hesitancy, I would say, "YES!" Those years were the most rewarding years of my life. Church work is hard at times; sometimes it's like a roller coaster with vast emotional ranges as you deal with people's heartaches and trials. There is no time card to punch; it's always a 24/7 of opportunities.

Because the workload was getting heavy at this particular church I was serving, the leaders decided that I needed an assistant. Doors of opportunity were open and I was able to secure a young man with whom I had worked in Christian television to come and work with me. Although "green" in some of the workings of a church, he caught on quickly and was doing a great job in helping to carry the load. I could easily say he was talented in many areas.

Now Todd was very tall and extremely thin, a perfect specimen of Ichabod Crane, bless his heart! He could hide behind me and I would never know he was there had I not heard him breathing!

One particular day, when our sick folks were in various hospitals scattered around the city, I had taken my assistant on our hospital visits as part of his training. Todd had not spent much time making these particular calls, especially on those who were critically ill and who might be terminal.

Our final visit of the day was to an elderly lady who was in ICU. Her family had nicknamed her "Big Bertha," although physically she did not match her name. She had always been a healthy, petite woman, whose appearance was truly one of a genuine Southern lady. Her makeup was always just right, not a jet-black-dyed hair out of place even as she lay on her bed, gravely ill.

She had several daughters, which to all standards of human behavior appeared to be normal. But as we know, in many families there is often one who stands out, different from the rest. Such was the daughter standing in the ICU with us.

Leaning over and placing her hand next to the side of her cheek shielding her mouth so Big Bertha couldn't hear what she was saying, she began to whisper. And then from this frail little woman, came her announcement, "I heard that! Careful what you say. I'm not dead yet!"

Giggling with a short snort because she had just been caught, the daughter (*trying to cover up*), turned to us and said, "Isn't she the cutest thing you ever did see?"

"Oh, cut the malarkey, Raylene, you're getting on my last nerve," barked Big Bertha, "and at this stage of my life, I've only got the one left! Now hush up so I can die in peace!"

"Oh, Big Bertha, you ain't going anywhere, darlin!" Raylene replied with her exaggerated southern twang, trying to encourage Big Bertha, but in reality, not wanting to face the fact that the end was near.

"Raylene, I'm 'bout to meet my Jesus, and if you don't hush up and let me die in peace when I meet Jesus I'm giving Him an ear full about you, and Shuga, you best stay down here as long as you can!" Then turning to me with a twinkle in her eye, she said, "Got any duct tape, Preachah?" Well, so much for my stereotypical "genuine Southern lady", bless her heart!

Little did we know at the moment that these would be Big Bertha's last words to her daughter, in fact to anyone before she crossed over. Looking around I couldn't see my assistant but I knew Todd had made his way from the other side of the hospital bed to take his stance behind me. I could hear his heavy, frightened breathing, a dead giveaway. (*No pun intended!*)

Regrouping her thoughts, Raylene started back in. Sadly, she said, "Between you and me, I don't think Big Bertha is . . . " and like a changing traffic light, "Like her hair color? Got it done a few days before," . . . and returning to her somber mood . . . "gonna make it!"

There was a moment of silence, with only the sound of the oxygen equipment and, of course, Todd's intense breathing directly behind me. Raylene suddenly broke the silence, nearly causing Todd to jump out of his skin (*not to mention my own heart skipping a few beats!*). Placing her handkerchief up to her mouth in dramatic fashion, she sadly expressed her grief as she leaned toward me. "Yes, I think Big Bertha is about to snuff out her last cigar. She's about to pass!"

From behind me, I heard a squeaky voice, reminiscent of my puberty days when my changing voice couldn't be trusted. "Pass? What do you mean 'pass'? Pass what? Gas, a kidney stone, going past 'Go' and not collecting 200 dollars?" Pressing my index finger to my lips and expressing a frustrated "Shhh!" I tried to quiet Todd's shaky voice. "Here in the south, that means 'died'. In other words, Big Bertha is about to die, or pass."

Raylene, unable to stay out of the conversation, began to add her "choreography". With her arm and hand, she began making an ocean wave movement, and explaining, "You know, crossing over, going over to the other side." Then abruptly she shot her hand up as if stopping traffic. "Pass, died! Get it, Yankee boy?"

When in doubt as to what to say, think, or do in such a case as this, I read some Scripture, had prayer with Big Bertha and said that we were just a phone call away, and we would be back to see her later. We had been encouraged by hospital staff to take some time away from the family since we had been with Big Bertha several hours and it didn't appear that death was imminent.

I dropped Todd off at the church to pick up his car and began my tedious hour-long drive in heavy traffic. The thought of getting out of my suit and tie and into something comfortable was quickly shattered by the phone ringing as I entered my home. It was Todd calling to tell me that the hospital had been trying to reach me, that the end was near, and we needed to return to the hospital ASAP.

I told Todd to get back as soon as he could and that I was on my way. It wasn't until I was speeding back down the freeway toward the hospital that I suddenly remembered Todd's response to me over the phone. He had stammered and fumbled for words before finally saying, "Okay!" It occurred to me that he had never seen a person die. Would he know what to do? Bless his heart; he was soon to be baptized into a situation totally foreign to him and without a clue as to how to handle it. I just knew he was going to quit, pack his things and move out of Dodge. In fact, he might not even stay long enough to grab his backpack before vacating me and everything else in his life. I even had a vision of a yellow "post-it" stuck to the end of the bed, "I'm out of here, Todd!"

Entering Big Bertha's room in the ICU, I quickly noticed that she was still lying in her bed, her spirit having departed. But where was Todd? I turned and started to leave the room and check in at the nurses' station when I heard that familiar breathing sound. Literally, across the room, hunkered down in the corner, on the floor in an upright fetal position, was my new assistant, experiencing a coma of fright, staring out into space. I must admit at the moment, Big Bertha looked better than he did!

Walking over to the corner, I extended my hand to pull my assistant up off the floor where he was shaking like a wet dog. "Are you all right?" I asked.

"That's the dumbest question you've ever asked me," Todd said with a small smile cracking across his face. (*I knew that later I would laugh at this whole incident!*) "Got any more of those up your sleeve?"

A few days later, arriving at Bailey, Banks, and Biddle Mortuary for the visitation, Todd and I was ushered into a small waiting room, being told that it would be a few more minutes as they were not quite ready. By this time Todd had regained his color and was laughing about the whole experience. "I'm good, I'm okay, I'm fine," he exclaimed, trying to convince me, but I knew differently.

It has always been my practice to be at the funeral home when the family views their deceased loved one for the first time. It's a time to bring comfort and support to the family. But this time, everyone, including the family and funeral home staff, was running a bit late. There we sat, in this small room with nothing but the slow and constant sound of a ticking grandfather clock. The ticking of the clock in the silence of the funeral home had all the markings of a good Edgar Allen Poe poem. Only the sound of a raven crying out, "Nevermore" could have made it any better.

I knew by the appearance and disappearance of his "Adam's Apple" on a regular basis, almost with the beat of the grandfather clock, that being in the mortuary was starting to get to Todd. I was afraid he had left all of his bravadoes at the door. Would I experience his curling up on the sofa into a fetal position again? Or would he start sucking his thumb or both? If he started crying out for his Mommie or worse yet, his blankie, I think (*figuratively, of course!*) I would have killed him on the spot before he had a chance to die on his own. I had already settled in my mind that I refused to cradle a grown man in my arms and rock him back and forth like a baby, just to calm his nerves and fears. Besides, how could you explain that to an undertaker if he were to walk into the room and see two adult preachers, one rocking the other in his arms? I know we men of the cloth are to show compassion, love, and support, but there's got to be a limit of how far we should have to go to fulfill our vows of compassion for all mankind!

The morbid door chimes of Bailey, Banks, and Biddle Mortuary sounded, adding to the already ghoulish atmosphere of the oldest funeral home in town. Its décor had to be the inspiration for the Haunted Mansion in Disneyland. Its old overstuffed furniture, its long century-old dark velvet drapes blocking any ray of sunshine, just added to the stale fragrance of flowers, past and present, even making the old "funeral veteran" like myself experience a moment of chills.

Taking one look at Todd, I instantly wished I had one of those harnesses mothers use to hook up their rambunctious children to keep them from running away. Todd's body language said loud and clear that he was expecting Morticia, Gomez, and Lurch from the Addams Family to enter our small room at any moment. If I could have moved behind him quickly enough I would have whistled the theme from the TV program, followed by the snapping of my fingers, just to add to his anticipation of doom and gloom.

I couldn't help but think of the horror music of "Night on Bald Mountain" and wonder what else I could do to frighten poor Todd. But alas, my scheming thoughts were shattered by the entrance of three elderly women, causing me to think I was seeing double, then triple. The mystery ladies entered the room, marching in single file in cadence with each other. They stood all of five feet each, and were identical triplets, not only in their facial features and build, but by the way, they were dressed.

Entering the room, they stood in front of the sofa, holding their purses with both hands in front of them. They were wearing brown trench coats that had seen many years of wear, mousy brown nylons which wrinkled down their legs and were met at the ankles by matching black orthopedic shoes. They wore their snow-white hair in buns adorned with black pillbox hats with small veils tenderly touching their foreheads. Their large pearl clip-on earrings matched their simple string of pearls. An extra layer of white facial powder covered their faces with two large gobs of red unblended rouge on each cheek. Their eyebrows had been plucked and drawn in with pencil, beginning just above the bridge of the noses, and making their way in a super arched curve beyond where their own God-given eyebrows would have grown, and stopping just below their temples, giving them the appearance of continual surprise at whatever was said to them. The three had picked up identical fans as they entered the building and were now cooling themselves in unison.

Much to my surprise and chagrin, Todd suddenly came back from the "edge of the grave" to ask a simple question. "What brings you ladies here to Bailey, Banks, and Biddle Mortuary, business or visiting?"

Immediately I knew he had made the wrong choice of words. Business? As if the ladies' backs couldn't become any stiffer, there appeared instantly and in unison, a look of indignation that could cut him in half if he wasn't careful.

With firmness that would rock the Rock of Gibraltar, Moleen (*who seemed to be the leader of the pack*) said, "Young man . . . " I knew then he was dead meat! "I beg your pardon?" As Moleen addressed Todd, I watched him slowly melt back into the shadows and I heard him say under his breath, "And I trimmed my nose hairs for this?"

"I'll have you know", she continued, "we're NOT here because we need the services of Bailey, Banks, and Biddle Mortuary. Although they've made quite a few changes lately, we still prefer the services of Alfonso Dawson Mortuary!" The words had been spoken with such finality; there seemed no possibility of disagreement.

However, Todd, feeling a bit more courageous since he had trimmed his nose hairs for the occasion, asked, "Why don't you like Bailey, Banks, and Biddle?" To my amazement there was a unified gasp, causing the picture of Jesus and the lamb on the fans to appear to have lost their balance due to the speed of their fanning.

"Ill tell you why we don't like this place. Our dear friend Lobelia passed recently," and right on cue they all made the sign of the cross, then kissed their hands in unison without missing a beat. "It was tragic, simply tragic."

For the next twenty minutes, Todd and I were "treated" to an expose of dear Lobelia's tragic service given by Bailey, Banks, and Biddle Mortuary. Everything from too much makeup on their friend, the botched obituary sent to the local newspaper, (Would they actually use the high school picture of this 90-year-old woman?), the misuse of the pink spotlight, to the fruit basket given to the family being "simply too small!" Even Lobelia's Alzheimer's disease was strictly the fault of Bailey, Banks, and Biddle!

The diatribe continued with, "It's beyond me how these undertakers can make a dead Episcopalian woman's face look like a star in a burlesque show!"O how I wanted to know how she would know how a burlesque star would look, but my better judgment squelched my question.

As I sat there and listened to these three ladies, although amused at their delivery and content of their speeches, I realized there was an element of truth in what they were saying, well almost.

By this time Todd was seated on the edge of his chair, his Adam's apple had reappeared, and he was glued to everything the ladies were saying. Observing that they had a new addition to their listening audience, they took full advantage to again promote their funeral home of choice which was NOT B, B, and B!

Listening to these ladies not only was interesting with sermon illustrations piling up fast, but it was helping pass the time while waiting to view Big Bertha. "Sounds to me, not wanting to pass judgment, that you have some legitimate concerns!"

"You nailed that one, Preachah!" Ileen said as if I had just discovered the fountain of truth. "Let me tell you, Sister Goosebe was one of us. . ."

"One of us?" I questioned.

"Yes, one of us! We all belong to the "Sisters of the Crossing of the Thames". . . Celestial City Chapter 333, and the Loyal League."

"Sisters of the Crossing of the Thames?" I again inquired.

"Yes! We're an international organization of women, formed with the purpose of building character in one another!"

"Oh, I see," I added with some doubt in my mind.

Gasping and holding her handkerchief up to her mouth, she continued, "I.... I mean 'we', pointing to her sisters. "We were simply mortified, I mean," and this time with an even more dramatic flair and gasping after each word, "Simply mortified." Quickly she added, "You know what I mean?"

"No!" I added with a dramatic flare of my own. "How mortified were you?" I gently inquired.

"Well, we were at poor Maria Goosebe's service, bless her heart. Yes, there she was in this cheap old cardboard casket (Visions of a Kenmore refrigerator shipping crate kept leaping into my mind!) that probably wouldn't even last till they got her in the ground. But that wasn't even the half of it."

She then proceeded to describe, or should I say verbally "assassinate" the preacher who had the audacity to show up for poor Maria's funeral. (Being one myself, I had been told not to take offense. No way would that happen anyway. This was WAY too much fun!) Her son had hired some "store-front Baptist preacher for the price of a bucket of Kentucky Fried Chicken". According to the family, the Hightower Primitive Baptist Church was one of those "pew jumping, snake spitting, slobbering, shouting, holy-roller-type churches." Anything not of the Episcopalian tradition was obviously considered by them to be "far out and to be shunned at any cost!"

But there was more. Fanning herself, and with a touch of pure gossip, she looked straight at Todd and continued crucifying the preacher. "For being a Hard-Shelled Baptist, he sure did sweat a lot! But aren't most Baptist preachers that way? Give 'em a piece of chicken, a biscuit and some sopping gravy and they can preach and sweat for another hour or two!"

Of course, the church was all wrong as well, having only a center aisle, so when the Bailey, Banks, and Biddle ushers, "dragged us clean up to the front, and to the second row no less," there was no way for them to get out if they found it necessary to exit the building.

Maria's two-hour funeral service finally ended (*and hopefully, the ladies' exposition of complaints!*) and the procession to the cemetery began. Fortunately, the graveside service was brief, as requested by the son. But obviously not brief enough! As the mourners were preparing to leave, according to the ladies, the gravedigger, who hadn't shaved for the occasion, wearing a pair of dirty bib overalls, his boots covered in mud, stepped up to the casket, placed a boom box on his shoulder, pushed the button and played the bagpipe version of Amazing Grace. "It was extremely humiliating!" With that, Moleen was finished.

I couldn't help wondering what was wrong with that! At least these Episcopalian mourners had a familiar song to send them on their way!

After all this discussion about poor Maria's service, bless her heart, I was more than happy to put my attention back to Big Bertha's visitation. The ladies were getting "antsy" as this visitation was putting a kink in their yard sale plans. They had spent the long winter months knitting all kinds of collectible items, and they couldn't allow someone's visitation to interfere with their sale!

I was completely taken back by their wanting to hurry things along and their lack of compassion. Did they think Big Bertha's family needed to check with them before she died to make sure it was a clear date? I'm sure she would have preferred not to have interfered with their sale, rather than dying with pneumonia!

Having heard the word, Ileen squealed, "Oh, blessed mother Maude! I'm not going in there risking catching pneumonia!"

Moleen, never one to allow the spotlight on someone else, had had it! "Pneumonia isn't contagious, you goon! Besides, you've had your pneumonia shot!"

With that, she straightened her hat, patted her hair bun, adjusted her coat, and sat back on the sofa.

"Thank you, Mrs. Kanazovich, for setting us straight on that," I said, clearing my throat profusely, realizing my tongue was in my cheek.

Quickly correcting the mistake, Moleen continued, "Oh, Reverend, I'm not married. None of us ladies are married." Her tone of voice gave no indication of whether she was sad or happy about the situation.

I soon realized these ladies were more like conjoined triplets than just sisters who resembled each other. Moleen had had a boyfriend in years past, but Leroy had become more than a little annoyed when the other sisters accompanied them on dates, of course, honoring Daddy's wishes. Nevertheless, the relationship developed into something serious and wedding bells were beginning to be heard. But alas, it all met its demise the night before the wedding when Doreen questioned, "And where are we all going on the honeymoon?" At this, the bridegroom jumped on his horse, rode into the sunset, and was never heard from again.

Evidently, the ladies had considered that they had entertained Todd and me long enough and it was time to take action

Moleen suddenly announced to me, "Sign our names in the guest register, if you would, please. We can't wait any longer. We've got a yard sale to finish getting ready," and they were gone; marching out of the room the same way they entered a half hour before.

Thirty minutes later the family arrived and we were told that we could go into the Slumber Room and view Big Bertha. After spending time with just the family in their time of grief, Raylene walked over to me and said, "Could you do me a favor?" Her request was that I get the funeral director and bring him into the Slumber Room because she wasn't happy with Big Bertha's makeup. By the time I had found the director and brought him into the Slumber Room, the damage had been done. Raylene, stepping back and admiring her work, addressed the director, "It's okay. I've taken care of it." Standing there viewing Big Bertha with the director, I held my breath, wondering how much of his fuse was left before it blew and I needed to take cover.

Raylene had taken her eyebrow pencil and drawn new eyebrows for Big Bertha, starting between her eyes at the top of the bridge of her nose, and going straight up at an angle, giving her that cat eye look. She then had taken bright blue eye shadow and applied it very heavily to her eyelids. Next, she had applied two silver dollar size gobs of bright red rouge, and layered her lips with bright barn red lipstick, outlining her lips with a black lining pencil. Her crowning touch was a Ginger Rogers beauty mark.

"You like it?" Raylene asked excitedly.

The funeral director rolled his eyes and shook his head in disgust, realizing indeed that he had not "seen it all" as originally thought.

Taking me by the elbow, Raylene gently led me to the casket, and again asked for a favor. "You want me to do what?" I proclaimed with fear and shock in my voice. "Shhh . . ." she whispered, handing me a twenty dollar bill. "All I want you to do is place this twenty dollar bill under Big Bertha's jacket and at the end of the service day after tomorrow, make sure it's still there when they close the casket for the last time."

I could feel the blood drain from my face at the same time a burning sensation ran up the back of my neck. "Let me get this straight. You want me to put that twenty dollar bill in her...jacket? Why place a twenty dollar bill in her clothes, knowing she's dead and in her casket?"

Her answer came quickly and surely. "Big Bertha never went anywhere without some money, you know, in case her car broke down, she had to make a phone call or something. So we want to make sure if she needs something while on the other side, she can always call home . . ."

"What are you doing," demanded the funeral director as he saw me pull back Big Bertha's collar and place a folded twenty dollar bill under her jacket. "You don't even want to know," I said, looking around the room and seeing Todd passed out on a sofa across the room being fanned by another funeral home assistant.

Once Todd came back to the living and was capable of walking, I took him outside to get some fresh air. Standing on the steps of the funeral home and without thinking, I said to myself out loud, "YOU CAN'T MAKE THIS STUFF UP . . . REALLY!"

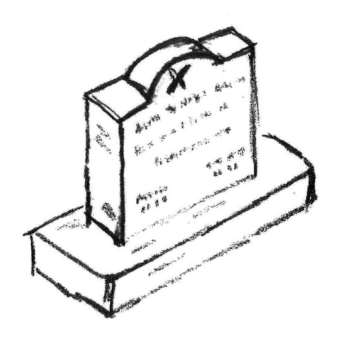

And I Thought My Family Had Issues

The sound of the car on the gravel driveway was a call to arms. Rushing to the front door and locking the storm door, she arrived in a flash. There she was, like a chained pit bull dog, teeth showing, deep throated growling, ready to attack. You could almost see her drooling at the mouth as she anticipated another royal battle, but this one would be the "mother of all battles".

Like the movie, "The War of the Roses", Annie and Henry's marriage started out on the wrong foundation. One could say it was almost doomed from the beginning. From all outward appearances, it was a one-sided romance, a marriage of convenience for Henry and a loveless one for Annie.

Lest we get the wrong impression of Annie, she was the most beautiful, caring, loving woman that you would ever want to meet, until you crossed her, or were disloyal to one of her close friends. We always joked that there were brains under those locks!

It was not beneath Annie to take you down with one of her famous "die-hard-head-locks" if she felt you were being disloyal to one of her friends. Many had experienced her encounter for this offense, always begging on their knees for mercy. The flip side of this loyalty meant she was not invited on many dates. Most men were afraid to go in for a good-night kiss, risking the possibility of finding themselves in that well-known position of being on their knees begging for mercy.

You just didn't mess with Annie and her friends. In fact, loyalty could have been her middle name, and why her husband couldn't see this is beyond human comprehension. Somewhere along the way, he had crossed the line and now it was payday!

"Let me in," Henry said as he pounded his fist on the door. "Open up!"

"You're not coming into this house with that woman! I won't allow it!"

Annie was adamant about "that woman" who had tried her dead-level best to prevent their marriage, and afterwards tried even harder to break it up."And now you want to bring that controlling, devious woman into our house? She couldn't stand me and the feeling was mutual! Are you insane?"

"Please, Annie, let us in!" Came Henry's reply once more, but this time a bit more forceful "before I break down this . . ." and the air became blue with his language. From here on things only got worse. Annie, yelling through the glass door that she wasn't going to let that woman into her house, with Henry pounding on the door threatening to break it down, all added up to the police being called...once again.

The neighbors were used to the yelling. In fact, when there wasn't anything good on TV that night, they watched and listened to the fight going on at 4200 Oak Street. When it appeared that blood or death was on the horizon, or if a certain sound level had been reached, compounded by barking dogs, someone would call the police.

The police didn't need to get directions to 4200 Oak Street as they had been there before. After exchanging salutations and "how are the kids?" the police began to fill out yet another domestic violence report as they questioned what was going on this time.

Knowing that the police were there to protect her if Henry was to try and break into the house with that other woman, Annie slowly moved to unlock the storm door. After explaining that this fight was about the other woman, the police asked that Henry leave her on the front porch as they stepped inside to discuss the situation. This was a disappointment to the neighbors when the police entered the house, because TV that night was reruns.

The police were quick to learn that there had been no physical abuse. Henry knew better than to monkey with Annie when she was mad, being fully aware of her capability of "die-hard-head lock!" Only verbal abuse, at which she could hold her own, was explained.

Once the police were informed of the other woman, they told Annie that she didn't have a leg to stand on as long as they were married and there had been no physical abuse. She had to allow the other woman into the house.

"Okay," said Annie. "But she's got to stay in the laundry room." After further arguing and displays of emotions, Henry consented to the arrangements for the other woman in his life that had brought nothing but grief into all of their lives.

I need to explain that the other woman was Henry's mother, now deceased, cremated, and whose ashes were residing in this little box he wanted to bring into the house. Although everything that had been said about her was true, it still was his mother. Being the only sibling that was anywhere near being sane, Henry had been forced to deal with her remains.

It all started when Henry received the call that his mother was in the hospital, very sick and that he had better come home, home being hundreds of miles away. Catching the first plane out he hurried to her bedside only to arrive too late. Her alcoholism and drug abuse had caused her body to completely shut down.

After the memorial service, and cancelling his return plane ticket, Henry decided that it would be best to drive his mother's car back to his home. After all, it was the cheapest way to go and there had only been enough money to cover the cremation services.

So, as previously arranged, the "Witch of Salem" was placed in Annie's laundry room. Week after week when she would start to do the laundry, she would see this small box next to the Tide, staring at her, until one day she couldn't handle it anymore. Reaching up and taking hold of her mother-in-law's ashes, she stood in the middle of the laundry room wondering where she could put this "old battle ax" where she wouldn't have to deal with seeing her on a daily basis.

Quickly she realized there was no better place for her mother-in-law than behind the washer and dryer. Seeing this room was a stranger to Henry, he would never be the wiser.

The marriage, as predicted, ended in a very sticky divorce, a lot of hurt and unheard of pain, dishonesty wrapping its ugly arms around lying and cheating. Left in the ashes of what could have been, were Annie and her two children.

Time moved on with Henry marrying several more times while forgetting that in the settlement of his first marriage, he had left his mother's ashes in Annie's laundry room.

One day as fate would have it, the dryer played out, and a Sears's repair man was called to fix the problem. Annie was at work, the kids were in school, and a key had been left under the outside door mat for the repair man.

Once the repair man had disconnected the washer and dryer, he proceeded to move them out from the wall. Noticing the small box behind the dryer, he stooped down and picked it up, thinking that maybe it had fallen down behind the machine some time ago, as it was covered in lint. Taking a closer look at the box he noticed an inscription written in bold black letters, "Such-and-such Funeral Home!" Almost dropping the box, he quickly set it down. But curiosity got the best of him as he slowly opened the box to reveal the contents.

Coming home early that day, Annie was just in time for the fun!

"Mrs., are you aware that there is a human body behind your washer and dryer? Do you know how it got there? And what do you want me to do with it?" came his shaky voice.

"Oh," cried out Annie, smiling to herself. "Don't worry about her. That's just my ex-mother-in-law. I forgot she was back there. It's been years since I put the old-battle-ax where she belongs."

"Yes, Ma'am," came a very nervous reply.

"I put her behind the dryer because it was the hottest spot I could find." (Thoughts of her possible afterlife came flooding in.)

"Yes, Ma'am, I understand."

"It's a long story, but don't worry about her, just set her aside and fix the dryer."

One can only imagine what the conversation was like when this Sears repairman got back to the shop. It probably was a first for him, and I'm sure he was hoping it would be the last as well.

To this day, I don't know if there was an extra charge on Annie's bill for psychiatric counseling for the repairman.

Time had healed the wounds of the sticky divorce that allowed her ex-mother-in-law to be placed once again next to the box of Tide. She would remain there on the shelf until Annie could decide what to do with her ashes, as her ex-husband wanted nothing to do with her as well. Maybe come spring she would spread her ashes on her Azalea bushes.

At Christmas time, out of nowhere Annie received a letter from Henry's sister. Annie knew it wasn't a Christmas card, so either she wanted money or was in jail and needed help with her bail. Opening the letter, she soon learned that somehow she had gone to rehab for enough time that she was thinking straight and wanted to know where her mother's ashes were, and if Annie had them.

"Would you please send them to me, since my brother Henry doesn't want them?" Weezer requested. "Oh," she added as an after-thought, "Merry Christmas!"

Being in no hurry, Annie got around to wrapping her ex-mother-in-law in a box and took her to the post office. Standing in a long line gave her time to reflect on all that had happened in her life, grateful that this was the final straw in getting rid of any evidence of the past.

"Next!" the clerk called out, dropping the box down on the scales. "Anything breakable?" he snapped.

"No," came Annie's response, knowing that she had wanted to break the old gal's neck many a time.

"First Class?" came the dull response from the clerk.

"No!" Nothing classy about this old broad, thought Annie. "Send it library rate!" That was the cheapest rate available at the time.

"Insurance? How much are the contents worth?" The tired clerk asked.

"Nothing! No insurance, contents not worth anything!"

"Can they be replaced if stolen, lost or not delivered?" asked the clerk.

"Thank God, not in this life time!" Replied Annie.

Watching the clerk stamp the dickens out of the box, sticking labels everywhere, Annie observed that the clerk tossed the box what seemingly was half-way across the room, landing in a mail cart, something she had wanted to do for years. When hearing, "Next," she began whistling as she walked away, her steps becoming lighter with each step she took; finally, the "old battle ax" was out of her hair for good!

WRONG! Christmas flew by and a new year began with the thought of no strings attached to the past, when suddenly one cold winter evening the phone rang. Much to Annie's surprise, it was Weezer, her ex-sister-in-law. She loved saying that word "ex!"

"Annie!" came the sharp voice on the other end of the line. "When are you gonna send me Mommy?"

"What do you mean, 'WHEN?' I mailed you Mother a month or so ago! You should have gotten her by now."

"You sent Mommy by parcel post? That's against the law to ship human remains in the mail," she yelled.

"Then sue me! Besides, you owe me four dollars and 95 cents for the old gal," Annie demanded. "Now, if that is all you want, I'm hanging up. I'm missing "Magnum P.I."

"No," yelled Weezer. "I sent you my address. Can't you read?"

"Can't you write?" returned snapping Annie. "I made the best out of what I could read."

"Look! I'm moving in a couple of weeks. Can you please go to the post office and put a tracer on Mommy?"

After a long pause, and not wanting to appear completely heartless, "Okay," Annie said, with a lack of compassion in her voice. I'll take my receipt and see what I can do, and if I find her, I'll send her UPS this time."

"It's against the law to ship human remains UPS as well," screamed Weezer.

"Okay then, you call a funeral home and pay the expense of transporting her back up to wherever you're going to be."

"UPS will be fine," chirped Weezer, suddenly counting the cost.

"That's what I thought," snapped Annie, hanging up!

More concerned with her love affair with Tom Selleck than talking with Weezer, Annie soon forgot about looking for her mailing receipt. It would be several weeks later before Annie would remember what she had promised. Another month went by before she headed out for the post office to buy stamps and check on the where-about of her ex-mother-in-law. After being redirected a dozen times to different counters, she finally found the right one.

"I'll take a book of stamps, and oh, I need to check on a package I mailed around Christmas time. It was never received," Annie explained.

Things were definitely not getting better as the clerk, a pimple-faced reject from McDonalds, now working for the U.S. Government, said, "Yeah, so what joo want me to do about it?"

Her first reaction was to reach across the counter and grab him by the collar of his U.S.-Government-furnished-shirt and give him a free lesson on how to treat the customer.

Handing him the receipt, she continued, "This package is missing. It never was delivered!"

"Was it a Christmas present? Did you meet our deadline promising delivery before Christmas," he spit out like he had been programmed.

"No!" Annie snapped back. "It wasn't a Christmas present... well; maybe you could say it was a present for me."

This only confused the young man further. Was it possible his only response would be, "You want fries with this?"

"You need to fill out these forms in duplicate. Make sure you print so we can read it! Where was it going?" he asked.

When she said, 'Maryland' you could bet on what the next question was coming from his unshaven lips. "Would you spell it!"

Thinking to herself, "I sure hope his mother sewed his name in his underwear. If not, this kid is doomed. He'll never find his way back home. But then, if I were his mother, that might be a blessing in disguise."

"What was the value?" he asked, twitching his chin and left eyeball.

"Value?" she replied. "You've got to be kidding! Nothing!"

"If it ain't worth something lady, why did joo send it in the first place?"

"I had nothing else to do. Listen!" Annie said through clinched teeth, as she shoved the forms, filled out in duplication, across to him. "Go in the back and see if you can find this package before I speak to your supervisor," wondering in her mind if he or she would be much brighter.

After what seemed like an eternity, "Boy Wonder" slowly made his way back to his station, dropping her ex-mother-in-law on the counter. "Is this what you've been looking for, lady?"

"Where was she?" Annie questioned.

Boy Wonder, without missing a blink of his left eye, said, as he pointed to an overhead sign that she had failed to notice, "Dead Letter Office!"

Instantly Annie went into a laughing spasm, unable to control herself.

"What's so funny, lady? It's just a box," Boy Wonder inquired.

"You don't understand," she said. "It's my ex-mother-in-law!"

"Your what?" he questioned.

"If you had read what I wrote IN DUPLICATE, you would know what was in the box.

It's my mother-in-law's ashes! You'll have one of these someday if you're lucky. Come and see me then and I'll tell you what to do with her! You can only be as blessed as I was to have one like mine, you know. It will be payback for your wonderful service."

Instantly, Boy Wonder turned ash white, (pun intended) as he hung on to the edge of the counter. You could hear the ripple effect of those in line behind Annie. "Ashes . . . ashes. . . ashes." Quickly she picked up the "Old-Battle-Ax" and hurried out the door before she could be arrested for the crime she had committed. But not before she heard this soft, scared voice cry out, "Next?"

Somewhere in the vast canyon of the UPS complex, going around and around on some conveyor belt, is Annie's ex-mother-in-law. If you find her, just leave her alone. She never could stand any 6-Flags rides, made her sick every time. Annie figures it's just a bit of revenge for giving birth to her first husband.

The moral of this true story is, be careful how you handle the remains of your departed love ones. You never know when they might come back to haunt you.

As for Annie, every time she sees a UPS truck, she stops for a moment of silent prayer, being thankful she's not married to Henry, and her ex-mother-in-law is out of her life for good. She only requests that when you see a UPS truck, you do the same. YOU CAN'T MAKE THIS STUFF UP . . . Really!

Green Bean Casserole...Again?

Iknew from the onset that this chapter was going to cause a whirlwind of contradistinction for authentic green bean casserole lovers. Others will applaud that someone has finally written how they've felt about casseroles for years, especially green bean casseroles drowned in mushroom soup and covered in dried onions.

Not being a casserole-loving individual, I learned early in my life that you can make a casserole out of almost anything! Slap a name on it; drown that baby in mushroom soup, and family members will think you got some gourmet recipe out of some fancy cookbook or from a cooking show on TV. From family reunions, funerals, births, Bar Mitzvahs, Bat Mitzvahs or any function where food is involved, and somewhere along the line a green bean casserole will show up.

I'm directing my comments toward any casserole, but especially singling out Green Bean Casserole (hereafter referred to as GBC) with mushroom soup and dried onions on top. Without much encouragement, my mind can begin to wander. What if ... you don't want to make it yourself? Not to worry, I thought. Go to Walmart and check out the deli, or K-Mart, aisle 7 back by the dog food. Buy a wedding gift and you'll find the bride is registered for GBC dishes at Target, and from the food section of Target, she's registered for several cans of green beans and . . . ! I need to get more sleep! A friend of mine was once asked to witness the execution of a convicted murderer. There under the execution table was his bowl of GBC! He took his casserole with him to the end. In this man's case, I can't say, "Bless his heart!" Anybody asking for GBC as part of his last meal on death row deserves what he is about to receive. I can't imagine leaving this old world and standing before your Maker with GBC with mushroom soup and dried onions on your breath!

Before I progress any further, I wish to make a certified, notarized statement that I do like green beans, fresh, frozen, and canned. I also like mushroom soup with those tiny bits they call mushrooms. So, if you want more bits of something, eat more mushroom soup, but keep it away from green beans.

I was introduced to the fine art of casserole dining upon being invited to a couple's home on numerous occasions. In my mind, it soon became effectively known as the Casserole Palace. I swear that sweet lady had every recipe that was ever invented for casseroles at her disposal (*and wasn't afraid to try them out, either!*) We would attend their home for a meal, and the buffet table would be loaded with various casseroles. Some actually tasted great to a "non-casserole man".

During my youth, I can remember that casseroles were not part of our mealtime experience. Remember, this was a time when there were no cooking shows on TV, in fact, any TV (at least at my house!) There was only one cookbook basically out on the market, unlike today, where there is even a cookbook on "How to Boil Water, 101!" (*Or the newer one, "How to Boil Water for Dummies"*). Our mother's filing system or cookbook was a drawer in the kitchen with bits of paper or 3x5 cards with family recipes on them, food sample smudges and all! I recall when my mother died I questioned my aunt about a certain dish Mom had made. Her reply, which might be strange to some younger generations, was, "I don't know what all went into that particular dish. It was all in her head. We never wrote things down."

Although time may have marched on, traditions surrounding funerals have mostly not changed in smaller towns. No matter where the location of the visitation might be, on the tables you will find fried chicken, coleslaw, potato salad, cakes, pies, and of course, banana pudding. Tuna casserole comes close to the top of my list of no no's for a funeral. Ever tasted tuna casserole that has sat out for two days? If the tuna doesn't get you, the mayo surely will. It's nothing more than increased business for the funeral home. (They love for folks to bring tuna casseroles!)

But wherever "post-funeral-food" is served, there needs to be a table set aside, marked "Green Bean Casseroles Only" with crime scene tape draped around the table, and a sign reading, "Danger, eat at your own discretion." And then, regardless of what denomination you might be, there should be a priest standing there offering "Last Rites" to those who blindly ventured beyond the crime scene tape and partook. A disclaimer would be a necessity, stating that the church or individuals who made the casserole are not responsible for any illness, seizures, or sudden or later death as a result of a GBC. And don't forget to have a notary public at the end of the table to certify the "Green Bean Casserole Release Form." If word ever got out, the CDC would have a hay day.

Actually, there is a history of the GBC which I should expound at this point if for no other reason, to be politically correct. I always thought GBC went clear back to the Garden of Eden, thanks to Eve. Then I thought it might have come over on the Mayflower with the Pilgrims. All were wrong assumptions. It was actually created by the Campbell Soup Company in 1955 as a way to sell more soup. Dorcas Reilly, the mastermind, was working in the Campbell Test Kitchen and helped invent GBC for an Associated Press feature article. Back in 2002, Dorcas presented the original 3x5 index card to the National Inventors Hall of Fame in Ohio for their display, smudges and all.

Some have even argued that GBC is actually on the five basic food charts. I added chocolate years ago, but not GBC!

But one thing for sure, GBC is a staple, crossing all

denominational and ethnic lines. This thought crossed my mind recently. Wouldn't it be surprising when facing judgment day, we find out that we had the answer to world peace within our reach and we completely ignored it? Green Bean Casserole to unite the world!

I have endured hundreds of casseroles in my lifetime at funerals, church potlucks, grand openings of Party City and Barnes and Nobel, just to mention a few venues, but this was to be the mother of all events! Fortunately, I have now lived long enough to be the founder of CA, "Casseroholics Anonymous."

It all started with an acquaintance of mine. He belongs to this church where the congregation is made up of elderly people, and when I say elderly, I mean ELDERLY. In fact, their church has oxygen tank hook-ups on each of the pews instead of hymnals. The assistant pastor is a certified registered nurse, and parking attendants are paramedics. In fact, the church bulletin doesn't have "upcoming events." They never plan that far in advance. It is not uncommon for him to attend 1, 2 or 3 funerals a week. I keep telling him that he should leave that church if he wants to live a bit longer.

This man is the most organized man I've ever met. Even his paper clips in his desk drawer are all headed in the same direction. He can walk into a public arena, stand there, look around, and within a couple of seconds tell me how many seats are in the place, how many skyboxes, etc. and I'm standing there thinking to myself, "Who cares?" Because of this unusual talent, (and his longevity up to this point), his church put him in charge of organizing the dinners for the relatives of the deceased, plus Wednesday night potlucks. They love to eat and tell lies, I mean, stories, about their past, "I remember when" potluck dinners. If there isn't an occasion, they'll make up one. Last week it was the changing of the light bulbs in the city hall parking lot, next week a repaving of a railroad crossing across town.

If you thought the paper clips lined up in one direction was unusual, you should see the sugar packs, napkins, and silverware on the tables. There was almost a split in the church when he started handing out Sweet & Low packets, giving additional ones to those he suspected might be "terminal". Then Cracker Barrel sugar packs started showing up, throwing off his count.

Some like to say he has the "spiritual gift of organization," to which his family would say, "Right. I don't think so! You try living with a man who counts every single sheet of toilet paper, per roll, making sure it matches up with the count on the package. Try standing in line with him at the Walmart service desk as he tries to explain that one particular roll of toilet paper was two sheets short and he wants a refund."

In all due respect to the man, he simply has an Obsessive-Compulsive Disorder that requires a neurological evaluation or a lifetime supply of Prozac for the remaining family members. God love his little heart!

When he gets the "death call", he springs into action, already calculating who should bring what, how many people to plan for, etc. etc. etc. He loves this kind of stuff! He immediately checks out who is officiating at the funeral service, his little black book telling him the average amount of time this preacher takes conducting a service, based on past experiences. Next, he calculates the miles between the funeral home or church to the cemetery, the location of the grave site, and how many steps from the hearse to the grave. Then he figures how many miles it is from the cemetery grave site to the church, and how long that trip will take, considering the time of day and traffic. He'll also know the length of time each stop light will remain red, and therefore he can determine within a fraction of a few minutes what time they will be arriving at the church. He'll know when to turn the coffee pot on, ice the glasses, and how many ice cubes per glass. He even knows what table to try and hide the GBC's. He's a master at this, like a well-oiled machine. It blows my mind while driving me up the wall at the same time. (If you're exhausted from reading all this, try living it. I speak from experience!)

The only hitch in this particular "after-funeral-dinner" was that he was short of help. Duh! What do you think of that? They're all dying off, and for pure entertainment, they all attend each others' funerals. They have to, of course, is their response. Yogi Berri put it this way, "Always go to other people's funerals, otherwise, they won't come to yours."

I was then asked if my daughter and I could help him out (at the very last minute). Surviving rush hour traffic (with my daughter at the wheel!) was a tall order in itself, but upon arrival, the orders started coming from my friend, the "Drill Sergeant."

Tables having been set up, the aroma of fresh brewing coffee and a roaring fire in the fellowship hall fireplace created a perfect picture. Those who had attended the funeral but not the graveside services had already placed their casseroles on the casserole table, making sure their dish was in the right location to be sampled first. Hopefully, they would receive the oohs and aahs as the tinfoil was removed for the entire world to see.

Assignments were handed out and I was placed in charge of incoming casseroles. I swear he was just getting even with me for something! My job would be to arrange the dishes, making sure there wasn't a bunch of one kind placed next to each other. Thinking to myself, one or two tables at the max will be sufficient, but to my amazement, a couple more tables were needed.

"Where do you want me to set my casserole, dear," she asked. "I could move Eva Belle's dish to the back if you don't mind, and place mine up front!" Leaning across the table, this sweet blue-haired lady, decked out to the nines, motioned for me to lean closer as she whispered. "If you're not in the mood for tasting death, young man, I'd stay away from Eva Belle's dish."

"Oh, really," I inquired. "And why is that?"

"Last time so many people got sick from eating whatever it was that she made, they had to call in a bunch of epidemiologists from the CDC to try and figure out what caused almost all of them to get sick. Willie Mae lost twenty pounds from the after effects from eating that stuff. (Actually, she could stand to lose another twenty!) CDC thought at first that someone had put anti-freeze in it, like the woman here in town who killed her old man by putting it in his food, but turned out there wasn't a single trace of anti-freeze in her casserole. So, be a nice boy, Shuga, and don't you dare move my dish, you hear?" Death threats in the church are the worst!

By now, the dishes were arriving fast and furiously as the guests from the cemetery had arrived. It was all that I could do to keep them lined up in their proper order while worrying about not offending one of the dear ladies.

"Hello, I'm Mizrus Bertha T. Butts," came the cheerful announcement as she handed me her casserole dish with her newly manicured hands, each finger covered in a bright jeweled ring.

"Mizrus Butts?" I repeated.

"It's pronounced, 'Bu-t'. It's French you know. The first 't' is silent."

Standing before me was this elegantly dressed genuine little southern lady, appearing to be something from the GONE WITH THE WIND era. Her lavender colored hair, from years of blue rinses, was coiffured to the highest possible height it could be teased and sprayed. (You know, big hair is still much in style in the south!) She was covered in what appeared to be a fortune in diamonds. She wore them everywhere, and only two things were missing. One was a tiara on top of her big hair and the other was a bodyguard for all of her family jewels she so graciously displayed, telling the history of each piece and from which husband it had been received.

"Here is my award-winning Green Bean Casserole, making its debut. This recipe has been in my family for generations. In fact, historians tell me it came over on the Mayflower with my ancestors."

"Oh, do tell," I said with a touch of sarcasm in my voice. "And how did you happen to come by this recipe?

"Ancestry dot com!" she proudly stated.

Leaning across the table, she whispered, "I'll tell you the secret recipe if you promise to keep it to yourself." Not giving me a moment to answer her request, she answered her own question and continued talking at a rapid speed. "You take two cans of . . ."

and before she got halfway into the details, she was repeating the complete recipe off the back of the mushroom soup can.

Next came Genneal, walking up to the table with her cherished casserole in hand. Re-adjusting the casseroles to suit herself, she quickly made sure hers was front and center.

"About that 'Butt's' lady," she said with a touch of disdain in her voice. "I saw you eyeing her jewelry, young man. Trust me, they ain't real diamonds. She got that fake stuff off that shopping network. You should see her house, stuff piled clear up to the ceiling with stuff she got off of that TV show."

Quickly finding the choice spot on the casserole table, she placed her dish down, but not without saying, "Betty Lou, that's Evan Crocker's widow, you know, the guy that died and we're having supper for! Between you and me, they didn't have two nickels to rub together. She loves my casseroles. Least I could do for her!" With a flippant wave of her hand, "Anyhow, it's just as well Evan died since he couldn't drive anymore anyway!"

And on it went, fussy old ladies, filling up the casserole tables with GBC's. I frankly had never seen such hostility as these women staked out their territory at the front of each table.

The only thing that saved the day was the long-winded pastor. Taking the microphone he started sermon number 42 which would be followed with prayer. Knowing I would have plenty of time, I started removing the tinfoil from the various dishes that had remained covered to keep them warm.

But Rev. Blowhard continued his rambling and I was now up to nine GBC's, and still counting! Eighteen, nineteen, twenty GBC's, in various shapes and forms, with only two small casseroles of scalloped potatoes, and no meat dishes in sight! I knew there must have been a sale on canned green beans (*or maybe mushroom soup*) down at the Piggly Wiggly!

But sad to say, tragedy had struck at poor old Evan Crocker's funeral potluck! My friend, who was always so organized, had failed to post a sign-up sheet the day before, and now look what we had to feed the multitudes. We needed something else besides GBC!

On the brighter side, well maybe? I hadn't realized how much variety there could be to this casserole. Genneal had mixed hers with Brussels sprouts, bacon, pineapple, peas, and tuna, even substituted mushroom soup with cream of potato soup. (*Someone had even put meatballs in their dish but it over-cooked and turned to mush!*) I did hear later that at the Minnesota State Fair someone was trying to sell fried GBC on a stick. Nasty!

All of this was going on while Rev. Blowhard was still praying until someone pulled the plug on the microphone. Did that shut him up? NO! As far as I know, he may still be in the church praying over dead Evan Crocker.

Meanwhile, the rest of the senior citizens had long since left the building and were wandering into "greener pastures". Across the busy four lane highway in front of the church was a pair of Golden Arches. Trying to get a mob of senior citizens across a busy four lane highway during rush hours, with walkers and canes, and some not even knowing which direction they were to shuffle toward, was quite a feat! Among them was Mizrus Bertha Butts of course, and remember the first 't' in her name is silent. It's French you know!

When she got halfway across the street she apparently stopped to adjust her "attire" at the same time a driver threw a lighted cigarette out the window. You guessed it, bless her heart. Gas Company said it would take a week or so to repair the road. I'll never forget her lying there in the middle of the road in her lavender blue hair and all of her shopping network diamond jewelry! She looked up at me and said, "Make sure you make the Green Bean Casserole with real mushroom soup and nothing but FRENCH Fried Onions on top!" She'll be missed!* (*I just made up this last part. She really didn't get hit by the bus, I just needed an ending. The sanitation department wouldn't approve of what I wanted to do with all those GBC's. Even they have standards!*)

*This chapter is a smorgasbord of ideas molded into one "casserole" of events from many experiences. Been to one, you've been to them all.

"Go in Peace...My Foot!"

Nothing could possibly scare the wits out of this individual in a hospital bed like being awakened from a deep sleep and finding a Catholic priest standing at the front of my bed giving me the Last Rites and I'm not Catholic! All kinds of things rushed through my mind at that instant. Did I have a heart attack, or should I have one? I didn't know I was that sick! Worse yet, don't tell me I picked the wrong religion a long time ago because if I did, I'm in big trouble!

No book in trying to cover all bases concerning the funeral biz would be complete if it didn't include at least one out of body experience, and if not that, at least someone's encounter with the Last Rites who hadn't gotten the memo, or heard, "check please!"

My Monday morning started out like any Monday morning, with my wish that God had started the work week at 12 noon. Although retired, I had always hoped someone would inform the sun that the day started at noon! As I made my way downstairs for fuel, trying to remove the fog that surrounded my brain, I wondered which Scarlett O'Hara philosophy in GONE WITH THE WIND would apply. "I'll think about that tomorrow" would work for starters. To my surprise, two large cups of coffee did get my engine started as normal

Stepping into the shower, I proceeded to scald my brain,

hoping that would jump start things, but I awoke twenty minutes later, finding myself on the shower floor, having fainted, bumped my head, and cracked the glass shower doors all to pieces. By this time, all the hot water had run out, leaving me the color of a bright red lobster. Only the cold water could serve as a wake-up call, bringing me to the realization that something must have happened.

Unable to stand up, I tried to slide my au natural body out of the shower in hopes of reaching my much-hated cell phone, now fast becoming my best friend... if I could just reach it. That six-inch step into the shower, which had never caught my attention in the past, now became Mt. Saint Helen!

Ever called 911 and experienced a logical conversation? Me neither. Here I am, "buck naked" being told by some 911 operator located some place in Hong Kong, to literally slide my bottom across the carpet (*Can you say, friction?*), go down twelve steps, and then unlock the front door and the storm door just after just fainting.

When I get them unlocked, I'm to hope no religious callers are on the other side about to ring my doorbell.

Then she kept saying, "You still there? Don't hang up! Help is on the way," to which I replied, "Can I request an all-male ER crew, no women?"

You would have thought I had asked her to drop by and wash my car. "Sir!" she replied in her snippy voice. "There's nothing they've not seen before!" To which I shouted back, "You want to make a bet? They haven't seen me!"

She didn't take too kindly to my reply. "You have a dog?" Having heard my affirmative reply, she continued. "Now I want you to try and catch the dog and pen her up." (*"Say what?"*)

Not only did this 911 operator want me to be arrested for public indecent exposure if there is an aluminum siding salesperson on the other side of my front door, she now wanted me to catch and lock up my dog who is not a biter, but a licker. I tried to argue but she wouldn't buy it.

So now in all of my glory, I was instructed to catch this wild dog who thought I was playing "Scoot, Scoot, Who's Scooting His Bottom?" In dog language she was barking at me, "You don't let me scoot my backside across the carpet, but you can?"

By this time I swear I heard the whole Rescue Squad Department in the county rushing to my house for show and tell! I managed to open the hall closet and spot a pair of shorts on the top shelves. Somebody with a sense of humor had to be looking out for me because there stood a yardstick that would help me retrieve something to put on. Oh, did I forget to tell you? It was the middle of summer, and these were wool shorts. Who in their right mind would buy wool shorts in the South?

Arriving in front of my house, announcing for all of the neighbors to gather at the curb like a bunch of vultures looking for prey, were not one, but four rescue units and one fire truck, lights a flashing. A total of nine men came rushing up on my front porch and into the house where they found my body dressed in a pair of wool shorts in the dead heat of summer.

Looking up at one ER worker I pointed my finger at him, trying to think of the right words to say that wouldn't offend him, and said, emphasizing each word, "Don't... even... ask!"

After all vital signs were taken and being hooked up with enough wires to launch me from Cape Canaveral, I was quickly loaded into a waiting ambulance. I thought I would have had my choice since there were so many emergency vehicles parked in front of the house, but I was assigned a driver from Israel, and his assistant from Paris, judging from their accents.

The Israeli, upon closing the back doors of the ambulance, said to me, "If he gets out of hand, just pop him one. That's what I do!"

GREAT! That's all I need at this time in my life, an Israeli driver who probably will drive like a frustrated Indy 500 race driver and a French man who thinks any moment I'm going to take a swing at him! Having been to Europe and experienced their driving skills first hand, I knew that I was in for a ride of my life and they didn't disappoint me.

There is nothing like flying down the interstate in a tin box on wheels, lights a flashing, siren blaring in the midst of rush hour traffic. If you've never ridden on a log wagon, it can only be compared to a ride in the back of an emergency vehicle. At that particular moment I was thanking the dear Lord they had strapped me down. Whipping in and out of seven and eight lanes of traffic, because some idiots won't pull over and make way for an emergency vehicle, would make the worst ride at Six Flags feel like a stroll through the park.

Upon arriving at the hospital and being ushered into the ER, I felt like I'd had a week-long experience of being pulled, poked, and drained of my precious blood. I was told I was being admitted, but there were no available rooms. So in the meantime, they would run some more tests, take more x-rays, and keep me from eating or drinking as a means of torture until the test results came back. I felt something very strange was going on each time they said "tests".

I recall when in school the word "test" meant you had to study first. Here you rattled off your name, date of birth, first and last child's name, showed them your ID bracelet and gave a pint of blood before they began the next test. I didn't have to study for one of those tests since someone else was assigned the work, when I was in school that would have been called cheating. All I could think of was that this must be what they call progressive education. Go figure!

Having not had a bite to eat since the night before, experiencing motion sickness, a ride to end all rides, enduring the pleasures of the ER, I finally fell asleep, only to be awakened at 2 a.m. I was not a happy camper! They had a room for me, not private, but a semi-private, with promises of a private room when one became available. After all, they explained, it was better than being stuck in the hall! Yeah right!

Not only had I experienced that ride to end all rides, Six Flags-styles when getting to the hospital, but now it was the "bumper cars" experience on the way to my semi-private room. The "gurney jockey", trying to steer my bed on wheels, appeared to be new at his job or was also suffering from a lack of sleep. There wasn't a piece of equipment in the hallways he didn't like, banging into each one of them followed by his constant comment: "Oof, that was painful!"

Thank the Lord for the baby crib side cargo bars on that gurney, or I would have been left lying in the hallway next to a crash cart. But then I got to thinking . . . Who gets discharged from a hospital in the wee hours of the night . . . unless it's someone with a tag on his big toe, and I was being put in that now-vacated bed? Worse yet, how many trips had this gurney made with someone whose big toe was tagged? I hope they changed the sheets!

By now it was 2:45 a.m. Do you know that is supper time for the late night shift? As a starving patient, try asking a staff member who smells like tuna fish and is trying to get something unstuck from between her teeth if you can have something to eat. Good luck!

But here I was, parked outside the door of my room, listening to the staff argue as they banged, and shoved stuff around in my room that was already overloaded with all kinds of equipment.

The man in the other bed, also not a happy camper, was awakened by the chaos, and to add to his misery, now wasn't being allowed to die in peace. Bless his heart!

You can rest assured that I had already put in my request for a private room before I arrived at this position. They promised to put me on the list for a private room when one became available. "First come, first served," was their motto.

Did I tell you they lie a lot? I was in a semi-private "torture chamber" for a solid week, observing patients being discharged, and being told I was next. At this point, I would have settled for a broom closet!

Now I've always been a person to have crazy things happen to me, unusual things, and things out of the ordinary. Perhaps it's just my lot in life! My mother, bless her departed soul, always said, "If there is a hole in the road some 500 miles away, you will find it and fall into it!" This hospital visit was my hole in the road, and I had found it! While explaining to friends any incident of this kind, I always seem to get, "Why doesn't that surprise me?" My middle name should have been "Murphy," for Murphy's Law. If there is any possibility that something could go wrong, it will go wrong!

Once the gurney jockeys concluded that they had room to maneuver my gurney into place, the attempt began. Murphy's Law was now in full action! The only comparison would be the attempt to land a 747 jumbo jet on the interstate! The curtain between the two beds was drawn, like someone marking a line in the sand and daring anyone to cross it, as if the poor dying man in the first bed gave a care. My observation of having my bed next to the window was suddenly shattered by this terrifying crash, enough to wake the dead, but it didn't in this case. One staff member backed into the dividing curtain, unaware that on the other side was the bedside tray cart, knocking anything and everything onto the floor. I just knew that noise would send that poor dying man on his way, with the help of possible electrocution as the water went all over his plugged-in equipment and on him, baptizing him in ice water. Ice water will instantly remind you of all your life's sins, for sure! Sad to say, the baptism didn't take. He was a Methodist and they sprinkle; this gentleman was almost drowned!

Of course, there was no, "beep beep" alerting the world that something was backing up. She just put it in gear, floored it, and that was all she wrote. She not only had had too many late night tuna fish sandwiches with Doritos on the side, but she was related to the ER gurney jockey. "Oof – that was painful!"

Finally tucked into bed, vitals taken, and "Can we get you something?" being said, which never happened, I was allowed to try and get some sleep. While lying in bed listening to the nursing staff laugh and carry on out in the hall, I begged Mr. Sandman to please comeback, but he wasn't answering his cell phone.

Suddenly without warning, my room became flooded with a brilliant light from the heavens. It had to be the angels coming for one of us; hopefully, it was the gentleman in the next bed because I hadn't had anything to eat in what felt like weeks. Not knowing how fast we would be traveling to the next realm, and having already experienced nausea from the ambulance ride, I was willing to pass. The thoughts of it being angelic were quickly shattered by a roar that shook the walls, causing me to know that it was coming from the other direction. It wasn't heavenly; it had to be a 10.9 earthquake.

Getting out of bed and going to the window, I quickly discovered the cause of the non-heavenly trauma I had just experienced. Outside my window was the landing pad for the "Life Flight" helicopter which was landing and had lit up the area like a Macy's Christmas Parade.

"What do you think you are doing?" came the panicked voices as a fleet of nurses came running into the room.

"What does it look like I'm doing?" By this time they had pushed my last button. "What do you think I'm doing? I'm looking at a helicopter landing outside my window that none of you warned me about, and then I plan on going to the bathroom while I'm up, and if you'll leave me alone, I'll try and go to sleep!" I thought to myself if I'm being too harsh on them I'll apologize tomorrow.

You would think I needed a government mandate to do something I had done on my own for years, or was I missing something? Was there a "Freshman Admitting 101" course for all those being admitted to the hospital and I failed? Was there a hospital instruction book that I first had to read to do what is a natural biological function? Did it come in the form of a child's book with pictures, God forbid, pop-ups, or was it "Mother, May I?"

By now, my head was spinning, my stomach was flipping from hunger pains, and they were putting me back in bed, lecturing me on safety rules of the hospital. They even had the audacity to hand me a Dixie cup for Mother Nature and me to experience together. These were educated, medically trained people trying to treat me? A Dixie Cup? Had government healthcare cuts gone too far? Go figure!

And we wonder why medical costs are running out of sight. To tell you the truth, it's cheaper to just die than it is going into the hospital for medical attention.

Obviously, hospital staff members don't talk with each other either. The only question they seem to agree on is, "Have your bowels moved yet today?" Every five minutes a different staff member entered my room and asked the same questions over and over. I got so tired of just rattling off my name and birth date every time someone would ask upon entering my "torture chamber," better known as a double room! I thought about inquiring about installing a "turn-style" at the door, but this wasn't the month for maintenance to work our floor. Hospital cuts!

How did I know they were actually hospital staff personnel asking questions? They all wore white jackets and carried their own personalized clipboard, like Moses coming down from the mountain carrying the Ten Commandments. The wad of ID name tags hanging from around their necks looked like they had spent a week at a summer camp in arts and crafts. They felt their ID cards gave them the authority to ask repetitive questions which by now were boring the spit out of me.

"Are you depressed or ever felt depressed?"

"No! Does it look like it? I'm in here because of an infection, not a mental health problem," quickly thinking that could be debated among some of my friends. My real thought was, no, but you are encouraging the possibility if you don't hurry up and leave the room with your dumb questions!

Her next question was the capping stone, "How you ever had thoughts of suicide?"

I slowly looked her in the eye, pausing for a great dramatic moment and replied ever so nonchalantly, "No, but I've thought of murder!" I don't know what got into her; she suddenly whirled around and left the room with her dozen or so name tags flapping in the breeze. I never saw this particular staff member in her white coat with personalized clipboard ever again. I would have given anything to have read the notes she placed in my chart concerning my behavior.

Now before you get the wrong impression of me, I am a compassionate person, but I ask you to place yourself in my shoes. Start with my collapsing in the shower, my 911 experience, camping out in the ER, and then trying to get into a room. Add a helicopter landing outside my window, experiencing government healthcare cuts with Mr. Dixie Cup, no sleep, and you'll understand my predicament.

By then it was 7:30 a.m. and all of the above, plus much more had happened in less than twenty-four hours. Now where was that lady with the clipboard wanting to know if I ever had thoughts of suicide? Now ask me!

I guess my attempt to tell them, "I'm not a well person!" had no effect. At this stage of torture, I was willing to say anything or do anything to get something to eat and some sleep.

Minutes later the overhead lights in the room suddenly shook my eyeballs to the back of my head as the room came alive in a blaze of glory. Who needs reveille when you have Nurse Scratchit's finger on the light switch?

More drawn blood, vitals, a clean Dixie cup for a new experience was fast administered. As if on cue, some teenager who appeared to have been up all night as well, brought in my breakfast tray. Hardly able to contain myself I pulled back the dome covering, hoping for what must be the most awaited delicate cuisine my eyes had ever observed. However, now it was my turn to ask the questions. "What's that?"

At this point, having not eaten in over thirty-six hours, I figured even the mystery food wouldn't hold me back. It could have been cardboard, but I was ready to dig in! At that instant, the bells and whistles on the equipment surrounding the bed next to mine went off, alerting everyone of a Code Blue. As the alarms echoed down the hall, a team of experts flooded the room and tried with all their training and modern day life support equipment, to save the gentleman in the next bed, but to no avail. For some reason, I suddenly had lost my appetite. Having observed every attempt possible, all I could say was, "Oof . . . that was painful!"

It was foolish of me to even ask, but I did, several times! "Where is my name on the list for a private room?"

After claiming they would check, the answer was always the same. "You're next!" But in what lifetime?

"You're next!" unfortunately didn't come fast enough. Roommate number two entered my life with his appalling gastric problem and I soon discovered he had no qualms about sharing it either. Surgical masks were the attire of the day, along with earplugs. Every nurse's aide who came shuffling her feet into the room seemed to take pride in announcing to the whole world, as if I didn't already know, "Boy, it stinks in here!" This always seemed to be followed by that cheap orange air freshener that coated the entire room and was almost worse than death itself. By now I was willing to have my bed rolled out into the parking deck, willing to have my own parking space, and would have gladly paid the weekly rate, just to get some sleep.

"You're next!" was fast becoming a serious problem for me and it was definitely no laughing matter. After observing patients being discharged and knowing I wasn't getting that private room, I knew I was willing to bring my own sheets and make my own bed, if they would just move me. Even this didn't faze them. So, being a God-loving, God-fearing Christian, I did the next best thing, thinking, "Act now, ask for forgiveness later!" I threatened to call in the Hazmat Team to address the issue of the problem in bed number one. It had reached that level of danger. If someone had struck a match, I wouldn't be writing this chapter. So I figured the appearance of men in aluminum foil suits, masks, and helmets, looking like they were headed for Mars, would get some action. It did! They moved him and left me with the false assurance I was on the waiting list and would be next.

Before the sheets could be changed on bed number one, I had turned off the alarm on my bed and was on my knees praying for the right roommate. I figured by now the nurses had had their fill of my asking to be moved and wanted some tender loving revenge leveled against me. At least I wasn't taking any chances. I reasoned if I could pray before Admitting sent someone to fill that bed, I could possibly supervene with some higher powers. After all, I did tell you that I'm not a well person! I know I told Heaven, hoping for any support I could get!

The capping stone of my prayers must have gotten a busy signal because before fresh ice water and a brand new Dixie cup could appear, gentleman number three arrived. I knew at first glance that "gurney jockey" was due a free "on the house" hernia operation, and that there couldn't be a single crash cart and other medical items in the hallway that hadn't been rammed into, damaged, dented, or permanently knocked out of commission.

Gentleman number three was of great volume in size and vulgarity, which almost sent me to the psycho ward without a reservation. His demeanor made me wish with every ounce of strength I had that I could bring back Rocky "Lady" Balboa in her white coat, clipboard, and dozen name tags and all! I would tell her I'd sign anything, do anything if she'd just get me out of this room. She wanted me to be depressed? Okay! I'll be depressed! Thoughts of suicide? I'll gladly trade "murder" for "suicide"...but upon quick analysis, forget suicide. I might need "murder" before I get a roommate number four. Trust me...it was bad!

Bed number one treated the nursing staff like they were dirt. I'm not casting stones, but was it payback time for the way I had been treated? Or could it possibly be payback time for something I had done in the past? Moving on.

Bed number one was also constantly demanding they jump to his attention the moment he pushed the call button. He was continually commanding something to drink, eat, etc., avoiding doctors' orders for "nothing by mouth" because of upcoming tests.

He made fun of my various items on my dinner trays while pushing his tray onto the floor if the items didn't suit him, claiming it was an accident. It was not beyond him to call out in the middle of the night, wanting me to get out of bed and change the TV remote for him. If I didn't, he treated me with the language of a sailor on leave. By now I had watched the nurses secretly turn off my bed alarm now that I had graduated from Mr. Dixie Cup to be able to walk on my own to the little boys' room with the help of an aid.

My first viewing of this gentleman was enough to cause nightmares for the next century. He was nothing short of a beached Beluga whale, wearing only a thong and weighing in close to 400 pounds. To say he sweat a lot is the understatement of the year. They had placed a free-standing fan on him blowing at full blast, causing the air in the room to circulate at almost to hurricane speeds, with the aroma convincing me he had no knowledge of soap and water. I was forced to bury my head in as many pillows as I was allowed to have before I checked out.

He became my worst nightmare. He hated life and anyone who had a life. It only became bearable when I had a "Come to Jesus" talk with him and Jesus wasn't present. As I was told on many occasions growing up, "You need an attitude adjustment, young man!" My talk was deeply appreciated by the nursing staff, for his treatment of them changed dramatically. But it didn't help move my name up to "next" on the private room listing. Win some, lose some!

Having the Mormon Tabernacle Choir standing at the foot of my bed, or an angelic choir replacing the helicopter outside my window, couldn't have been more welcome than the news that roommate number three was going downstairs for tests and would be gone most of the day.

Quickly entering into a sleep-induced coma, I went deeper than I had in days. Sleep was now my new best friend. How long it lasted is unknown; regardless, it was not long enough. What shot me up and out of my deep sleep, is also unknown. However, it was devastating.

Shooting straight up in bed, faster than NASA sending a rocket to Mars, I yelled at the Catholic priest standing at the end of my bed who was at that moment giving me the Last Rites. I didn't know someone could stutter while making the sign of the cross, but the priest almost fingered himself to death.

"What in blue blazes do you think you're doing?" I screamed. "Did you even look to see if I had a toe tag?"

I've always heard that in those final fleeting moments of

life, your whole life can flash before your eyes. Such was not my case at that moment; it wasn't my life on this final PowerPoint demonstration; it was also not the much-talked-about "tunnel". For whatever reason, my "flash before your eyes" contained no "tunnel". Someone had goofed! There wasn't even a light (which would have been at the end of the tunnel), no previews of what was on the other side, no floating above my death bed, no one telling me to go back because it wasn't my turn to go just yet. Instead, just an elderly priest whom I appeared to have sent into a shell-shocked coma at the foot of my bed.

There appeared to be no time for me to yell out, "Oops!" or even, "Oof, this is gonna be painful!" I must have made a wrong choice years ago in selecting my religion. Or did I? Something was drastically wrong with this instant flashback thing since there was no tunnel. As a young person, I always wanted to be Catholic, not for religious reasons, but because they didn't have services on Sunday evenings and that was when Gunsmoke and Bonanza were on TV. Had mother been wrong in raising me in the wrong faith, and now as a last chance to repent, a Catholic priest was here at the foot of my bed before crossing over?

I know my yell was loud enough to break the sound barrier, but I was unaware of its power of sending a priest almost into cardiac arrest. Losing his balance and falling back up against the wall, dropping his prayer book and his vestment sliding from around his neck, his facial expression verified it all. He couldn't believe what he had just performed. Now he and Jesus had much more in common when Jesus said to a dead Lazarus, "Lazarus, come forth!" He had to know within his own mind that he was guaranteeing himself sainthood because he had raised someone from the dead.

As he picked himself up off the floor, along with his prayer book, I tried to think if my rising from what he thought was dead, ranked right up there with seeing the Virgin Mary on a cheese sandwich or the face of Jesus on an old oak tree? Did it rank right up there with the appearance of the Virgin Mary down in Guadeloupe, Mexico?

Trying to explain to a faint-hearted priest that I was a Baptist was a project in itself! "I'm Bap . . Bap . . . Bap" I tried to explain! Stuttering and spitting over every word that tried to leave my mouth would hopefully be enough to convince the priest that he wasn't dealing with someone who had gone rabid.

"Are you "so-n-so"? the shaken priest asked. "NO!" I yelled, having been conditioned by the entire hospital staff. "I'm Kenneth, birthday, etc. . . etc . . ." throwing my left arm up in the air pointing to my wrist band for verification.

Upon hearing the priest announce the name of the individual he was looking for, I pointed to the empty bed next to mine, "It's him! May I suggest you give him a double dose of whatever you're delivering? NO!" I quickly added. "Make that a triple! He needs it!"

"I must have gotten into the wrong room," he stuttered as he looked for the list of names he had been given. You think? I thought to myself.

After regaining my own thinking powers, and coming out of a sound sleep, "Are you all right?" I asked the elderly priest, knowing he had fallen. Straightening out his vestment, he finally answered my question, "What in blue blazes do you think you're doing?"

His shaking voice, apparently not only from Lazarus (*me*) coming forth but possibly from having several cups of communion wine before encountering me. It seemed quite clear at the moment that he needed something stronger to calm his nerves. Gaining his composure, he explained how he had been notified that the individual in my bed had died and that he was needed to administer the Last Rites offered by the Catholic Church for the dying or deceased.

After the Catholic priest had left, a nurse came into the room to apologize for the mix-up and for any stress it might have caused me, and for the unpleasant stay I may have had. May have had? I thought to myself. She done bumped her head if she thought this had been Club Sunshine. I could tell by her face that she wanted to say something but was a bit hesitant to begin.

Drawing a big breath, she informed me that my roommate's

tests that day had revealed he didn't have long to live and he was being transferred to a different wing of the hospital the next day.

The good news was that the doctor had signed my discharge papers and I was free to go home. She then paused, drawing a large breath and said, "A private room has become available. Do you want it?" I guess the look on my face spoke more volumes than I care to explain. And she administers medication, narcotics? Observing my facial expression, she quickly added, "I take that to be a no?"

I once read, "Comedy is tragedy plus time!" It's the unique capability to take tragedy that we all experience in life and help others to see the other side of human tragedy, humor. I've always believed if you look hard enough, you can always find something to laugh about, or at least smile about, in every life experience.

Upon checking out later and leaving the room, I passed my roommate who now was back.

The demanding mouth that had cursed me out numerous times said, "Go in peace!" as he made the sign of the cross. My only response was to the orderly pushing my wheelchair, "Keep moving!"

"Dear Lord, Why Didn't You Call Me to be a Plumber?"

To borrow a phrase from Charles Dickens, "It was the best of times; it was the worst of times." This would certainly describe the 1960's. Richard Nixon became President, the Vietnam War was in full swing, and Generation X was born. America had faced the assassination of President John F. Kennedy in 1963 and now must encounter the assassinations of Attorney General Robert F. Kennedy, and civil rights giant, Martin Luther King, Jr. We all stood as proud Americans observing the achievements of Apollo 7 followed by Neil Armstrong's walk on the moon.

It wasn't a time of innocence, but political correctness had not yet entered the American mind. It was a time when we simply enjoyed life and didn't have to walk on eggshells, afraid of offending someone. When it came to the Halloween season, we had fun, and didn't try to make it into something it wasn't!

Some might find it hard to comprehend this chapter because times have greatly changed and we can't simply enjoy a Halloween party without being accused of some demonic activity. Some indeed have taken a simple activity and added horror and gore beyond belief.

Yes, things were different in the 1960s and 1970s. But go back to the 1940s and 1950s to reinvent the word DIFFERENT! No TV (at least at my house!), no video games, no hanging out at the mall.

We made our own entertainment and Halloween was the best! I remember my mother taping cutout black cats on the front door, having taken time to cover them in paint that glowed in the dark. I won't ever forget the cardboard skeleton, also covered in "glow in the dark" paint. It took no less than two (maybe more!) weeks to plan our costumes in order to make them "just right". And candy corn was the candy of choice. It seemed the day would never arrive when we could go pick out our pumpkin, but then there was more "waiting" for another day to carve it out. Once the pumpkin was carved, then black and orange crepe paper streamers were hung in preparation for scaring the Trick or Treaters. Can you believe we went house to house for 2 or 3 nights in a row, filling our sacks with all kinds of candy, popcorn balls, cookies, and candy apples? Our parents never had to check our "loot" before we could try a piece! Oh, it was a time of innocence all right—OUR innocence!

My co-author's parents and mine were good friends and attended the number one Sunday School class at our church. Their Halloween parties were the highlight of the season. (Yes, it was a Baptist church, you who are gasping!) The Beaver Class party each year had the judging of the best costumes, best-carved pumpkin, best dessert, etc. They even bobbed for apples. (Any of you Millennials even know what that is??)

But alas, I soon became a teenager and the tradition of Halloween grew even more important for me, as in writing major productions for the youth group, still in good taste and in the spirit of just plain innocent fun. One of my fond memories was when my mother helped me create a casket. I had obtained a large cardboard freezer box, brought it home, and (kindly, of course!) asked my mother if she would help me. She cleared off the dining room table which soon became the center of the season work table. Mother took the time to cut the box down to size, painting it, and even lining the inside with cloth. It looked SO authentic sticking out of the trunk of my dad's car, ropes and all! It would take "center stage" at our youth group's Halloween party! Oh, how I miss those days for my grandsons, a time they will never know!

But time marches on, and Halloween began to change. I was now an adult, with my schooling behind me, and I was hired as an assistant pastor in a church, in charge of the youth. This was indeed the "best of time," working with this youth group in a small farming community where the young people had wonderful values, had been taught respect for each other and their elders, and appreciated whatever was done for them!

The teen program at the church was like nothing that had hit the community before, and our numbers were exploding. Kids were coming from miles around to attend our activities on Friday and Saturday nights. Sundays were busy with morning church and a 6:00 p.m. Bible study, followed by the evening service. (How unique was that? A Sunday night service?) After service was always a kind of "afterglow", fellowship in a park somewhere or at someone's home, with food, fellowship, and a challenge for the coming week. (Were they as tired as I was at the end of this kind of day?? Probably not!) Wednesday night brought another Bible study. There was always some sort of activity to keep the kids busy and serving . . . mission trips, traveling musical groups, weekend retreats, summer camps and much more. My philosophy was to keep them busy with fun activities, teaching them along the way how to live the Christian life, and somehow overcome the stigma of the word "church".

I knew it was of utmost importance to plan something special for the kids for Halloween night, keeping them active, or I (*and the town!*) might suffer the consequences of their boredom! As our grandparents had experienced, "farm youth" could get into a whole heap of trouble pulling their pranks!

Halloween prep began in August with the help of the two married couples who would help fulfill my vision. Many a time their eyes would nearly pop out of their heads when I presented the idea for an activity, but (*bless their hearts!*), they were willing to try anything once! When I presented my "Spooktacular" Halloween plans, their response was predictable. I could almost read their minds: "He's done gone and bumped his head this time." One of my lady advisers always sat there laughing and saying repeatedly, "O my Lord, how in the world are we going to do that?" Her husband would shush her and tell her that I had everything all planned out and for her to be patient. She would soon say, "Let's do it!" with her husband ready and able to jump in with any building issues which were needed.

I didn't sleep much that night after the first planning meeting, but when I did, I slept fast. "Spooktacular" was going to blow the socks off of this church, and the town! I was going to authenticate that I had indeed bumped my head!

And the church people's reaction? Already they were thinking I might have a screw loose and nobody was willing to get close enough to tighten it up! Never mind the "We've never done it that way before!" folks who hadn't had a thought outside the box in the last 50 years! But then, with having the largest youth group in the history of the church, one would find it hard to argue with success.

Of course, you can't have a "Spooktacular" without going to a "spooky" place. The local funeral home! Pulling into the parking lot like someone was chasing me; I surprised Mr. Mitchell, the director, who was watering the flowers. I could tell that my actions didn't surprise him one whit. He was like a grandfather to me and we had spent a lot of time together. Actually, I had helped him with so many funerals that he asked if I'd like to move into the apartment that was attached to the funeral home. I moved in and out all in the same afternoon! To be perfectly honest, it scared the wits out of me, just knowing that on the other side of that thin wall lay someone who wouldn't be cracking jokes with me come midnight! The annoying fragrance of "bygone posies" which permeated the place 24/7 was no comfort!

Turning off the water, we went inside and had a cup of coffee. Now you've never lived (*no pun intended!*) until you have a cup of funeral home coffee! It will flat out knock you down while taking the varnish off the woodwork at the same time.

I explained my Halloween plans to Mr. Mitchell, and in doing so, I could see these two kindred spirits were on the same page.

Grinning from ear to ear, he ventured, "What do you need?" After explaining the details and making a list, everything seemed to be falling into place. The only problem was that I needed a real casket, not something like my mother had made years ago out of a freezer box. A REAL casket for these sophisticated (*streetwise, although of the rural variety!*) teens who wouldn't be fooled by a fake box!

A new casket was out of the question—WAY too expensive for our budget! After another cup of varnish remover, Mr. Mitchell remembered that out in the garage (*where the hearses were kept shudder - shudder!*) was a shipping casket. This amounted to nothing more than a cheap wooden box, a shipping crate, which looked like a REAL casket and was covered in gray material. Just the ticket!

Once we got the casket down out of the rafters, I had to ask a foolish question as we removed the plastic dust cover. "Where did this come from?" Mr. Mitchell smiled as he opened the lid, and slowly said, "It's used." My simple reply was "Get out of here! You've got to be kidding!" But on closer examination, "Eeooo. There's makeup on the pillow!" Without batting an eye or saying a word, he reached into the casket and turned the pillow over. "There!" was his solution to the problem. "All fixed! Now you can lie down in it!"

ME, lie down in that "used" casket??? I don't think so!

But my curiosity was about to kill this cat and I couldn't resist asking, "But why did you keep this pine box?" Now with a smirk on his face, he replied, "Because I knew that sooner or later you would be looking for one, so I kept it for you!"

I knew I couldn't lick a "gift horse" in the mouth, but now who could I get to lie in a used coffin? Sure wasn't going to be me as I have previously stated! Hmm. Was there someone I wanted to get even with??? I could always tell him/her after the fact that it had been "used" previously.

To be completely honest, I was on the verge of asking myself if I had gone too far this time. I had thought it was a great idea, but now, I didn't know. My self-questioning was interrupted by a phone call from some of my parents who wanted to bring their teenage daughter and have a talk with me. Now what, I thought, but then reminded myself that these were supportive parents and reasonable in the dealings I had had with them in the past. Surely it couldn't be anything too serious, could it?

They arrived a short time later and after small talk, the dad spoke up. "As you know, our daughter has a heart condition, but since she first heard about "Spooktacular", she has been keeping us up nights begging to be a part of it. Can you tell us what is going to happen?"

Asking the young lady to leave the room, I explained the activity, the details of which had been kept under wraps until now. I assured them that we always had a registered nurse at our outings and adult supervision was of the utmost importance to me as well as the church. Among the details, of course, was the need for someone to lie in the USED, shipping crate style casket. After she came back into the room, all was explained to her and immediately she jumped at the chance to play this important role in the production. The girl, her parents, and the nurse all agreed to absolute secrecy and swore not to tell ANYONE of the plans!

As I walked down the hall, I "high-fived" anyone who would cooperate! I had my living corpse!

My next job was to find a "haunted" house, not just any house, but exactly the right one! I had spent literally hours driving around dusty old country roads looking for that house that would tie everything together. After almost giving up, I came upon this old, deserted farmhouse that was perfect. It oozed of Edgar Allen Poe, Vincent Price, and Boris Karloff, the masters of horror. It was a two-story house, had broken windows, was in need of paint, and was almost too far gone to be repaired.

After walking through the house in daylight, I couldn't help but have chills just wondering what it would be like in the complete darkness of night! The rooms were connected in a perfect pattern for movement, and the house even had that old smell, perceived by some as being haunted. Olfaction in its finest form.

After receiving permission from the owner of the property, we began turning the house into a "Haunted House." Establishing a pattern for walking through the house, we began to turn every room into something different. We didn't have to work too hard as there was no electricity—Everything would be scary in the dark! It even came with its own cobwebs, one less thing for me to worry about!

We had the usual "haunted house" paraphernalia, but two favorites of mine were different. In one of the upstairs rooms, we covered the floor in old bed springs and placed mattresses on top, making it unstable to walk on. Then we hung thirty-five old tires from the ceiling, a few feet off the top of the mattresses. The teens would enter one doorway and have to go completely across the room to exit another door. Once they stepped on the box springs and the tires were bumping into each other, it was almost impossible to get across the room without being knocked down. Once out of that room they would be faced with a long curved staircase in order to get down to the first floor. The only problem, we had enclosed the steps in large freezer boxes, making it into a large sliding tunnel, landing at the bottom on old mattresses while being hit in the face with flour! One room was an autopsy room with a few "bodies" lying around and plenty of (*fake*) body parts to pass around. In the field next to the house we made our own graveyard with tombstones, etc.

By the time Halloween arrived, my youth leaders were on board and understood where I was coming from. "Spooktacular" was the talk of the town and we knew we had a "hit" on our hands. Even the "naysayers" were asking what they could do to help. Money, food, and candy corn were pouring in and everybody wanted to be a part of the action. Advertisement and excitement caused us to go to not only a ticket requirement but to add a third night. Tickets were going like wildfire!

Having the Thursday night "Spooktacular" under our belts, and feeling great about the next two nights, I was walking on air, along with the youth team leaders! Those Scriptures "...Take heed lest he fall" and "Pride goeth before a fall" SHOULD have at least crossed my mind. Not! I was soon to learn their true meaning!

The plan was to start the festivities at the church in the fellowship hall, which now had the appearance of a genuine funeral home. To set the mood, we had borrowed a hearse from the funeral home and had parked it outside the fellowship hall. Cars with adult drivers were lined up behind the hearse, with any teen drivers placed in between the adults. Men in black suits, dressed like undertakers/zombies, with white face makeup and large black circles around their eyes, worked the parking lot, especially for crowd control.

Upon entering the fellowship hall, each teen had to sign the guest book as requested at any visitation. The only difference was that the pen was hooked up to give a gentle shock to the writer and which caused a multitude of screams. The lights had been turned down low, with two pink lamps on either side of the casket. The flowers consisted of dead weeds and soft organ music played in the background as the teens were ushered to the front and were greeted by the "grieving" family dressed as the Addams family. As dry ice floated across the floor, the "deceased" would occasionally rise, uttering her moan, which brought on more screams. You just can't have a Halloween funeral without low-flying fog!

The service itself was filled with fun stuff, slapstick comedy routines, a mad scientist, walking dead, etc. At the conclusion of the service, the teens were placed in cars lined behind the hearse. Destination unknown—as all details had been!

Everyone was impressed with our police escort to the haunted house. Yeah, I knew what was ahead at that house (*spooky sounds, flashing lights!*), but if I hadn't known, you wouldn't have gotten me in that house!

The teens arrived at the haunted house and had a riot going through it. Unknown to them, I had a stranger dressed as a policeman, drive up to the house, flashing lights and all. Rushing out, they were surprised to see a law enforcement officer way out in the country, but they gathered around to hear what he had to say. He announced that there had been an escape from the mental hospital that was located a mile or two from the farmhouse.

Everyone was to go back inside and wait for further instructions as to when it would be safe to come out.

Of course, I had to be brave, being their "fearless leader." I suggested we tell ghost stories while we waited. Suddenly, right on schedule, there was a terrible noise of breaking glass coming from the basement area. Immediately, the room went silent. So silent that it was deafening. Showing "extreme bravery", I cautioned them to not say a word or move. You could have cut the fear with a knife! After a long pause, and returning to our ghost story, a second crash was heard, this time from upstairs on the second floor. Suddenly a man appeared at the top of the staircase, obviously the man from the mental institution. He slowly descended the staircase, giving orders to everyone not to move, with his gun pointed directly at me. With a surge of adrenaline, I made a leap forward trying to take him down. The gun went off and he ran out the door and across the field, as I grabbed my stomach and fell to the floor. Unknown to the teens, I had a bag under my white shirt filled with watered-down ketchup, and a needle attached to my ring. Upon sticking the pin into the ketchup, I then pressed against it making more liquid to come out, making it look like an authentic gunshot wound.

The plan had been to yell "Gotcha", to laugh and joke that I had pulled one over on them, then go back to the bonfire where hot dogs awaited. But sometimes the best-laid plans don't go the way they're supposed to! Three of my loyal teenage boys sprung into action. "He's been shot! Keep him warm!" Before I could say it was a joke, these teens picked me up and placed me on the floor. Should I continue to keep up the charade or jump up and blow my cover?

Unknown to me, two of the teens who were track stars, took off running about a mile and a half down the dirt road to the nearest farmhouse to call the police and an ambulance. (*No cell phones, of course!*) One thing I had failed to do (*on purpose*) was to tell my youth leaders about the ketchup and the mental inmate. Now they were concerned! "Keep Pastor warm. Give me your sweatshirts, cover him up."

The shocker of all shockers, came when one adult leader said, "Hang in there, Pastor. Tom and Gary have run to the nearest farm. They'll get help!"

"HELP?" I yelled as I tried to get up, only to be pushed back down. "Lie still, you've already lost too much blood!" What everyone didn't know was that the local police department had put all funeral homes on alert that night and told them to listen to their scanners, just in case they were needed. When Mr. Mitchell heard the distress call, he immediately informed the police that it was part of the "Spooktacular" and not a real emergency.

Returning completely out of breath, my loyal track stars tried to comfort me by informing me that help was on the way. The others huddled in small groups, waiting and wondering what would happen to their fearless leader who tried to save them.

One of Mr. Mitchell's hearses was also used as an ambulance and was equipped with flashing lights and sirens. This served as quite a spectacle as he came racing down that dusty country road, lights flashing, siren blaring, heading to the wounded youth pastor!

When Mr. Mitchell pulled into the front yard, some of the teens ran and opened the back door of the ambulance, planning to pull out the stretcher. Much to their surprise, it was loaded with cold soft drinks, hot dogs, and potato chips for a real bonfire feast. The look on their faces was priceless! I just crossed my arms, stood up, and yelled, "Gotcha!" A split second after the shock had worn off, I was attacked by my senior boys and down I went with them on top of me. Before I knew what was happening, I was picked up, dropped into the used coffin I vowed I would not lie in, and the lid CLOSED on top of me with the thud of three heavy bodies sitting on top of the lid! OOPS! BACKFIRED!

"Grave-ly Funny: Hilarious Obituaries"

Whether covering several pages in a small hometown newspaper or a few lines in a large metropolitan newspaper, the obituary column can be a place of tribute to a loved one, with warm words of regards, inspirational stories, or even hilarious moments. But lest we become too sentimental, it can also be a battleground for a "Custer's Last Stand" of revenge between siblings and those who have longed for the last word concerning this departed relationship.

There is also a trend of those writing their own obituary on their way out of death's door, a form of self-expression, provided a family member doesn't edit it down before it reaches the newspaper office. Here is some of our favorite out-of-ordinary obituaries collected. Names and locations have been omitted to protect the innocent and the not so innocent.

– Let's begin on a high spiritual note . . . well, maybe not so high with "No Regrets." The writer of this obit lifted a line from the Life Application Bible which said, "He passed away, to no one's regret." (*2nd Chronicles 21:20.*) His obit read: "No one was sorry when he died!"

Don't you wish in some of these incidents you could proofread your obit before someone had it printed? For example:

- "(*Name*) bought the farm last week (*died*), having lived more than twice as long as he had expected and probably three or four times as long as he deserved." (*I'm sure this wasn't meant to be a compliment!*) It went on to say, "Many of his childhood friends who weren't killed or maimed in various wars became petty criminals, prostitutes, and/or Republicans. Deceased was a daredevil: his last words were 'Watch this!'"

- (*Could one say, "Anyone have the phone number of a good fumigator?*) "She leaves behind a brother and 117 cats." (*And a large cat food bill!*)

- (*Don't ask me. I don't get the connection either!*) "His hobbies were, hunting, NASCAR, football, and WELDING!" (*I guess you could say he was versatile?*)

- (*A man after my own heart.*) "A lifelong love affair with bacon and more . . ."

- (*You can't live in the south without having a family member, or an old dog named Bubba. It's a "rite of passage!"*) "His family affectionately called him Pork or Bubba." (*Deceased*) is remembered for his sense of humor. He was a devoted animal lover. (*I'm not kidding!*) He is preceded in death by his relatives and pets: Buster, Lady Bonkers, Silky, Susie, Daisy. Survived by the "light of his life" his (name) fiancée and his only child, "Thunder child!" (*The obit went on listing a dozen or more names: aunts, uncles, cousins, along with all of their "nick-names." Obviously, they left someone out on a previous obit – OR – they're a tight-knit-family?*)

- (Deceased) obituary in the (*newspaper*) included practical advice she learned over the course of her 102 years of life: "Floss daily, give nice presents, homemade candy is delicious, speak your mind, work hard and always carry a hanky."

- *(I've often wondered this myself...)* Andy Rooney once said, "Why are caskets so decorative? If you're inside them, who cares what they look like on the outside. I don't understand."

- *(It appears she got the last word in . . .)* "I (deceased) a comely, loving and long-suffering bride of 47 years, died on *(date)* from a touch of lung cancer. Now that I know smoking is not harmful, I probably got it from a bad ice cube! My ashes will be scattered at sea, my meager estate paying for the wake, which is the only way anyone would attend. In lieu of flowers, a donation to *(name)* can be made. Since I've had a ball in life, with no regrets and nothing left still undone, and since our world seems to be quickly deteriorating, it's a good time for me to cash in. Goodbye, and good luck!"

- *(TMI Too Much Information!)* The sun rose for *(deceased)* on *(date of birth)* and his home going celebration will take place tomorrow when the sun sets. He is survived by his wife, *(Name)* who was a good wife, who was faithful and devoted to her man, "too devoted," if you ask me. She got a wakeup! She never stopped caring and doing good things for him in spite of. *(Deceased)* was a good man, a jealous man, who needed anger management classes. Jealous over his women!

- *(Name)* moved a lot. He dropped out of high school and was later diagnosed schizophrenic, and got his GED. He inherited his love of music from his parents, particularly his mom's side, the drums. He could and was a great impersonator, mimicry, especially Richard Burton and Richard Harris. He tried acting and comedy, but these efforts were thwarted by his wild side. He was an extra as a football fan in the bleachers, in the film starring Matthew Mc Conaughey. *(A bit of information in case you want to look the film up and spot (Name) in the bleachers.)*

— (NAME) was a member of (Name) Church and Masonic Lodge #? A retired tree cutter and sewing machine mechanic. *(If you figure out how these two relate, let me know!)* His many talents and hobbies included traveling, reading, singing in church, playing poker, and savoring a good glass of red wine and telling bad jokes. Survivors include his dogs, Jackson, and Parker, his cat Mr. Jones.

— *(So sad, no family members to miss him?)* Dearest Busia will be missed by his beloved pets who brought him great joy: Zinnie, Okie, Cleveland, Vino, Gracie, Zip, Oscar, Oshie, Rosco, Flash, and Kozi.

— *(What a trooper)* (Name) may have had many courageous battles with this or that disease, but wanted you to know that he lost this battle. It was primarily as a result of being stubborn and not following doctor's orders or maybe for just living life a little too hard for better than five decades. He would like to thank all "his ladies," *(Are you sure this isn't what took him out?)* for putting up with him the last 30 years. During his life, he loved to hear and tell jokes and spin tales of grand adventure he may or may not have had.

— *(Oops!)* (Name) is survived by her husband and his companion. *(I wonder, did they sit with the family during the service?)*

— *(Yay team! To the bitter end!)* (Name) respectfully requests six Cleveland Browns football players to serve as pallbearers so they could let him down one last time.

- *(I'm only reporting!)* In lieu of flowers, please do not vote for *(said)* Politician!

- (Name) was a scrawny, long-bearded moonshiner, with a foul mouth and a passing acquaintance with copper tubing and kettles. He was the embodiment of moonshiners of yore gone by, died. Over the years he had brushes with the law and was first convicted of selling untaxed liquor. Sorry to say, he had a bad encounter with a bad batch of hooch which wasn't taken too lightly by some folks. *(You don't mess with longtime customer's hooch and expect to survive.)*

- *Revenge at its finest played out in a well-known newspaper between siblings and their opinion of the passing of dear old mom. It all started by one of the siblings placing the original obituary in the paper, followed by other family members comments . . . side by side!*

- *(Headlines read:)* "FAMILY FEUD PLAYED OUT IN THE PAPER"

(Deceased) had no hobbies, made no contributions to society and rarely shared a kind word or deed in her life. I speak for the majority of her family when I say her presence will not be missed by many if any. Very few tears will be shed and there will be no lamenting over her passing. What all of us will miss is what we never had, a good and kind mother. *(OUCH!)* There will be no service, no prayers, and no closure for the family she spent a lifetime tearing apart.

The opposite right-hand column, same page, read:

The survivor is self-centered enough to believe the obituary is about him, as appears to be the case with

93

(Name). He placed an obituary for his mother (*Name*) who died on (*Date*) taking the opportunity to insult his siblings (*Daughter*) and (*2nd Son*) with the following: "She is survived by her Son (*First son*); who loved and cared for her; (Daughter) who betrayed her trust, and (younger son) who broke her heart."

Then the next day this followed, the daughter and younger son wrote their own obituary for their mother, against the oldest son: "(*Name*) drained the mother's savings and maxed out her credit cards. The (*older son*) used their mother's Social Security checks to go on a vacation to Branson, MO. and Alaska. *(This could be material for another reality show!)*

— *(Nothing like telling it as it is. Short, sweet, and to the point.)* (NAME) was in an automobile accident, he lay there while medical personnel worked on him, while whimpering, and telling jokes, cussing, begging for narcotics and bargaining with God to look after his wife and kids. During his life, he excelled at mediocrity. He loved to hear and tell jokes, especially short ones due to his limited attention span. He died at the hospital on Tuesday. Sadly he was deprived of his final wish which was to have a double date with his wife, Rush Limbaugh and Ann Coulter and to crash an ACLU cocktail party. His tombstone was to read, "Fred who?"

— *(Deceased name)* wrote his own obituary that was short, one paragraph in length, but you could tell that he had been a character. His service requests appeared in his obituary, stated: "A caravan of grave-digging friends and well-wishers are expected to provide funereal talent, shovels, sweat, cheer, graveside manners. Eulogizers of quick-witted brevity are welcome to speak. Long-winded downers may be stoned and used as backfill."

- *(The following obit had to be edited from its original content and length. My guess is that some revengeful relative, or a friend playing a last minute joke, we'll never know, must have written this large epistle of information. We only printed it because we needed filler to make this chapter longer.)*

- "*(Deceased name)* was a dangerous-charming southern boy who managed to graduate from high school with 1.6 average and enduring 13 mind-numbing years of public school before enlisting in the war, after divorcing *(name)* his wife of six years formerly, his step-mother for 12 years – he then moved to a different state and took up promptly with a former babysitter from his grade-school years. This was two weeks after Mt. Saint Helens' historic off-topping. *(I'm exhausted already!)*

  A short few years with the *(city name)* garbage collection squad he went into roofing and siding contracting. Not having enough activity in the romance department, he joined the Unitarian Church which had a very active singles group with a surplus of women 10 to 20 years his senior.

  (Hey! At this obvious age, you can't be that picky!)

  During a doldrums period of employment and romance, he attempted to enter the medical field as a nurses-aide, as this proved, after all not a good fit, as he felt compelled to take half of his charges home to provide more adequate personal nurturance, while the remainder, he felt, should be taken out over-night and shot.

  Several years later he claimed to have found his calling as an arborist, and changed his legal name and attempted to make an honest living in taking care of trees. It was later when pruning an ancient apple tree for a frugal-but-charming Southern matron; (deceased) met his second-wife-to-be. It was a mere 8 years later before she caught (*deceased's*) eye and they were married on the Autumnal Equinox at a pot luck affair. The next nine years passed in what appeared to be sublime, flawless bliss, until (deceased) noticed a mild, chronic sore throat, and some difficulty swallowing. The symptoms persisted, eventually revealing a tumor in the advanced development, which directed (*Name*) to thoughtfully and humanely end his tenure."

— PETER THE CAT whose ninth life ended on (*Date*) was a well-known cricket watcher at Lord's, where he spent 12 of his 14 years. He preferred a close-up view of the proceedings and his sleek, black form could often be seen prowling on the field of play when the crowds were biggest. He frequently appeared on the television screen. It was said of him, "He was a cat of great character and loved publicity." *(Hey! I'm not making a comment! I'm a dog lover!)*

— *(You won't believe what some people will do to get time off.)* Headline News screamed:

"Man Submits Fake Obit for Mom to Get Time Off"

A 45-year-old man took playing hooky from work to a new level by submitting a fake obituary for his living mother to a local newspaper. (*Name*) sent an obit notice to the local newspaper to get paid bereavement time for his job at a local factory. *(Just when you think you've heard it all.)*

The newspaper editor (*name*) says he accepted the obituary in good faith, but after being unable to confirm the funeral arrangements at press time, according to the AP, the son's plot was then exposed. When the employer found out, he was then fired from his job after the newspaper reported that his mother was alive and well. *(Wouldn't you have loved to have been a fly on the wall after his mother got done with him? You probably could guarantee one less seat at the Thanksgiving table!)*

— *(As a southern old-time preacher would say toward the conclusion of his already long sermon, "Now before I close..." This last obituary is fairly long, but not as long as it was before I took my pen to it. Here is an example of a genteel southern lady, knowing her time was short, decided to write her own obituary. She was known for a gentle, yet sharp wit, and could spin a yarn to the point you believed every word of it. How much of the following is true? We'll never know. That was the gist of writing her own obituary. You gotta love her for facing the edge of life with a smile on her face. Oh, P.S. I truly believe it wasn't the disease that took her; she died from total exhaustion if she did half of what follows. Honestly, I'm not making any of this up; her pre-written obit reads as follows.)*

— The (deceased), fully aware that her struggle with cancer was quickly approaching the edge of earthly time, would not allow it to steal her faith nor wit, began to write her own obituary and instructions. When the time came friends and family were awed at her composure as she was now secure in the arms of our Savior. One of her final requests was that her head was to be comfortably and attractively tilted at about a forty-five degree angle so that her head symbolically is resting on our Lord's right shoulder.

Miss *(name)* was born with a strong and unique sense of humor that allowed her to contribute her own unique touch to her obituary.

Miss *(name)* was born and raised in *(name, deep south)* a cotton mill town populated with very few fine old families of respectable lineage. Fortunately, this family enjoyed the benefits of sterling flatware at holidays and the general satisfaction that comes with knowing who one's people are.

Miss (*name*) showed an early interest in music. She held a piano performance degree and was equally happy putting her talents to use in the piano bar as she was at various churches.

Moving to New York City she pretended to pursue a career in theater but it soon became apparent that she was too lazy for a theatre career.

After two years as a Telex operator, Miss (*Name*) took a position with the American Red Cross. She resigned after nine months due to the fact that she was about to be fired.

After fourteen years in (*Northern state*), Miss (*Name*) moved to (*Name*) to attend a Theological Seminary in preparation for ordained ministry. She managed a few semesters before realizing what a terrible mistake she had made and quit full-time study.

Miss (*Name*) enjoyed so much quitting something. Quitting was an activity she had come to love and would enjoy for the rest of her life

Sadly, she stopped making homemade mayonnaise and began to put dark meat in her chicken salad, but she did remember how to set a table. While in (*City name*), Miss (*Name*) met her long-time companion, Miss (*Name*), with whom she would share many lovely vacations and several questionable real estate transactions.

Moving once again, Misses (*name and name*) moved out west where she enjoyed being employed seven years by the Department of Corrections. Though unable to convince anyone to give her a weapon, badge, or pepper spray, she loved working for "The Department."

She was a woman who made people laugh in the face of death! She was picking out her urn online and laughing about whether she should get a keepsake urn. She said she was not a particularly thin woman, but had doubts that she should fill more than one urn!

She wasn't afraid to die. She was looking forward to it as the next great adventure.

I Wore a Suit for This?

Last night was one of those nights where I knew I needed to get some sleep but couldn't. So I turned on the TV while lying in bed, which is a "No! No!" especially for me because if I watch a comedy I will get myself so worked up laughing that it is all but impossible to go to sleep afterwords. Such was the case as I watched the outlandish American classic, "Arsenic and Old Lace." I still laugh as hard as I did the first time I saw it.

Take two doughty little old ladies, gentle spinster sisters, Abby and Martha, who poison lonely old men as "one of our little charities!" Of course it's done in the best of taste, with their homemade elderberry wine! Lest we judge, they have nothing but charity in their hearts for the lonely. Add their brother Teddy, who thinks he's Teddy Roosevelt, digging the Panama Canal in the basement, and you'll leave with a nutty fruit salad of comedy that'll make you scream with laughter and shiver with excitement at the twists and turns in this zany and fast-paced comedy.

Sitting straight up in bed, I yelled, "That's my character description in our next chapter!" If you can picture this true account that follows, with its two main characters, plus one, as Abby and Martha, you'll catch the full impact of the story. These two ladies leap off the screen into the real live characters in this chapter.

Over the years I had had the privilege of visiting these three gentle spinster sisters,(well, all but one was gentle!) in their home. There was Hettie Mae, who was completely deaf, but loved to sit and smile while throwing me kisses upon my visits. Then there was Lula Jane, the spitfire of the three and definitely the leader of the clan. For some reason she never did like preachers and wasn't afraid to express her feelings, refusing to even open the front door when they tried to visit. But for some reason, that all changed when I suddenly became their pastor. In her eyes, I could do no wrong. Thus the other two sisters had to fall in line with her thinking as well.

Then there was the third sister, who for some strange reason was always called, "Sister Raymond!" Nothing else, not sister, not just Raymond, but always, "Sister Raymond!" Unless you addressed her in conversation in that way, she would not respond.

They lived way out in the country in "no man's land." Their house sat at the top of a large hill surrounded by numerous trees. From the hard road you couldn't see their home, just a long winding road. But they knew when every car left the hard road and started up their drive, greeting any possible visitors with loaded shotguns, and they knew how to use them. Hettie Mae, although deaf, would be pointed in the direction of the approaching car, and she could pick a flea off a hound dogs back without disturbing the dog.

Their home was so clean you could almost eat off the floor. With nothing out of order, it was like stepping back in time with all the furniture covered in plastic for protection. It had the mixed aroma of mothballs, lavender, and Ben Gay. Sometimes if they knew company was coming, there was an added aroma of over-powering "Ben Hur" perfume, $1.00 a gallon at the Dollar Store.

Protocol was the order of the day. No matter what they were doing, it always had to be done in order and led by Lula Jane! Come Sundays, they would get into their large Buick Roadmaster, vintage 1960, with Lula Jane driving, Sister Raymond in the front seat passenger side giving directions, (although they had been to church hundreds of times), and Hettie Mae in the back seat. Not seated on the left, nor the right, but squarely in the center. They would enter the sanctuary at 10:45 a.m., (not 10:50, or God forbid, 10:40 a.m.), go to their regular pew, and pity anyone, including a visitor, who happened to be seated in their pew. Should some poor, unsuspecting soul blunder into their private territory, the "ousting" procedure was the same. They would stand single file in the center of the aisle, Lula Jane, Hettie Mae, and then Sister Raymond. They would not say a word, but clearing their throats in unison, they would glare until the message was received.

They always wore hats, (*never to be caught off the farm without one!*) two piece suits, white gloves, and their purses draped over the left arm, freeing the right hand to hold the bulletin. Tasteful vintage jewelry was always the crowning touch, but the pancake makeup covered a multitude of "aging sins".

As the years passed, it was obvious that they were all three starting down that slippery hill of failing health, but especially Hettie Mae. The day arrived when there were no longer three sisters, but two. No more walking in single file, assigned seats in the car, protocol at the kitchen table. Hettie Mae had stepped from this old earth of pain and sorrow into the ever loving, waiting arms of her Lord and Savior, Jesus Christ.

True to form, every detail of her funeral had been outlined prior to Hettie Mae's passing. All I had to do was show up.

The funeral home they had chosen was one of the most beautiful ones in the area. Once you left the main road you turned onto a long estate-type winding driveway past beautiful greens, reminding one of a well-manicured golf course. There were fountains, drop dead (no pun intended) gorgeous flower gardens, tasteful statues, all having the appearance of a country club rather than a funeral home. Had I known I was driving into such luxurious surroundings, I would have gotten the hot wax car wash rather than the "just hose it down!" look!

I was met by a team of funeral home personnel who, upon learning I was the Clergy of the Day, started treating me like royalty. Some even extended their hands to shake mine, to which

I reluctantly reciprocated, but thinking, "I wonder what they touched last? I hope they washed their hands well."

Ushered into the large lobby, I saw in front of me a large flat screen TV with the listings of all the deceased, with pertinent information for each. There, appearing next to Hettie Mae's name was mine! First time I had ever seen my name in lights, and it had to be in a funeral home!

Being quickly taken into the Clergy Room, I became aware of my own personal "attendant", waiting on my every need. In fact, I soon would have to think up "needs" in order to keep him busy! The bathroom? Definitely too pretty to use! Linen towels and a tray of expensive toiletries, all for my enjoyment.

But for the moment, the door opened and in walked a gentleman who looked more like the head butler than a funeral director, who announced he would take me down to see the family.

As we walked toward the visitation room the funeral director took me into the chapel. Right before we got there, he remarked, "I'll show you our little chapel and where you'll be standing before we meet the family."

I felt like shouting Gomer Pyle's "Shazam!" when I stepped into what the funeral director called "our little chapel." It was short one or two bricks of the cathedral in the wedding scene of "The Sound of Music." "Gol-ly," I said to myself, trying to decide if I should burst into, "The hills are alive with the sound of music," or just stand there with my mouth open, catching flies.

After taking in all the magnificence of the Old World opulence of history past, this cathedral, in the midst of a large city, would have appeared out of place had it been anywhere but nestled in this serene setting. There was a certain reverence in the silence of this marvelous cathedral they referred to as "our little chapel!"

After staying in the silent "reverence" of my surroundings for as long as I dared, I knew I had to leave and greet the family. Walking into the crowded visitation room, I stood in the doorway looking for Lula Jane and Sister Raymond. I had only taken a few steps into the room when I heard in stereophonic voices, one from each side of the room, both sisters, loudly announcing, "Preach-ah." As long as I had known these sweet sisters, they always had called me "Preach-ah!" Never an "er" on the end of "Preacher," but always with a southern flare. "Preach-ah!"

The two little old ladies toddled over to where I was standing in the middle of the room, wrapping their gloved hands around my waist and resting their soft heads on either side of my chest. Almost like someone had given them their cue, they both in unison reached up and patted my chest as they led me to the casket. "You must see our sister! She looks wonderful," softly said Lula Jane, with Sister Raymond repeating the same words.

As if I had a choice, (*which I didn't!*) I felt two little hands in the small of my back, pushing me toward the casket. "Go up and see her - she ain't got a wrinkle in her face . . . Oh, they've done such a good job." Sister Raymond repeated, "Not a wrinkle, not a wrinkle! Good job, good job," and then she puckered up her lips, released them, then puckered back up again.

I knew it had been some time since I had seen the sisters, but I noticed instantly that Sister Raymond was, as they say in the south, slipping very fast. She wasn't her vibrant self as I had remembered. She was indeed the female version of Dustin Hoffman's character in the movie, "Rain Man," repeating every word and action of her sister Lula Jane.

"Isn't she the most beautiful thing you've ever seen, Preach-ah?" proclaimed Lula Jane, with Sister Raymond repeating every word.

Lula Jane was right. Hettie Mae did look lovely, as lovely as a person who has passed can look.

"Notice," said Lula Jane, again repeated by Sister Raymond, "we put gloves on her. Not only does a genuine lady wear gloves when she goes out in public, but no matter how good these funeral home people might be, they still can't make the hands look normal!"

Before I could slip away from Lula Jane and Sister Raymond and allow someone else to hear how she died, and how beautiful, etc. Hettie Mae looked, I had to be shown one special floral arrangement. It seems there is always one arrangement that the family feels came straight from heaven's shores, when in reality it is the tackiest thing in the room. You can't have a "gin-u-wine" southern funeral without one.

It's usually a square sheet of Styrofoam with some ribbon wrapped around it. Placed in the center is a toy phone with the receiver off the hook, and surrounded by plastic flowers. The ribbon displays, written in glitter, "Jesus Called and She/He answered."

If anything will crack me up at a funeral, it is one of these arrangements. It's not that I'm making fun of the situation; it's just the classless look it represents among all the other beautiful flower arrangements. It always looks like some first grade art project, or the WMU ladies' group from down at the Baptist Church who took time out from rolling bandages to make this creation.

Sure enough, I gave an Academy Award performance as I was shown this home-made creation, knowing Jesus hadn't called. Be assured that in this electronic age with all of these fancy cell phones, there was no way Jesus would still be using such a tacky rotary phone to make His phone calls, especially something from the Dollar Store!

"Don't you think she looks right purdy, even youthful?" Lula Jane said, only to be repeated by Sister Raymond. I put my hand up to my lips and raised my eyebrows to cause wrinkles in my forehead. (*Don't worry; the overhead pink light took care of most of them!*) And without saying a word, I turned and left the room, but not before I received sympathetic pats on my back from Lula Jane and Sister Raymond. Is it my fault that they misinterpreted my attempt not to laugh for grief?

Walking out into the hallway, I was stopped by my personal attendant who most graciously said, "Reverend, would you follow me, please?" He took me into a side room where he proceeded to remove face makeup from my suit obtained from hugging various guests. "Mus'nt have our minister looking tacky. Care for a cup of fresh coffee, soft drink, water? Can I get you anything?"

"No thank you," I replied. "I think I'll take a walk back over to, (quoting) 'your little chapel'. I still have time before the service." I couldn't help but think that within a short period of time, James the Butler would no longer be at my service, and I would have to step back into reality.

Just as I walked back into what I called the "cathedral", my ears were assaulted by the most piercing sound, echoing even louder in the vast canyon of the cathedral. Was it their smoke alarm? Was there a fire somewhere? Had someone who had passed just arrived, and like the general store where Pawpaw always shopped, there is a bell by the door to ring if you enjoyed their service? But this was a siren. Did we need to evacuate the building and if so, where was the nearest exit?

But my train of thought was quickly interrupted as ten or more funeral home employees came running from all directions, almost knocking me down. They had turned from extreme funeral home servitude into Firemen of the Year. "Everybody out immediately!" Their actions could be compared to arranging the deck chairs on the Titanic. No one knew what he was doing, at least from all outward appearances.

Not smelling smoke for the moment and looking around for the nearest exit sign just in case, I stood back to watch this "organized chaos" unfolding before my eyes.

Flying down the hallway in lickety-split speed on the verge of needing traffic lights if nothing else for safety reasons, was a string of caskets being pushed by anxiety-filled funeral home attendants. Where they were going, no one knew. All I knew was that they were getting these bodies out of Dodge.

To tell the truth, it was quite amusing as I watch that bunch of "wild turkeys", who only moments ago had tried to act so dignified, but now were in a full-fledged panic mode. They must have rehearsed this procedure because every guest was ushered out of the building in a formal fashion, even the steady stream of elderly people leaving the building, walkers and all. "Organized chaos" had now become organized without the chaos. (*Thus the need for gold pins with their names engraved?*)

Stopping one of the funeral home attendants as they attempted to fly by, I proceeded to question him. "Does the funeral home have a water sprinkler system?" The blank look on his face should have been enough of an answer, but not thinking clearly, I proceeded further. "Okay, then. Is there water falling from the ceiling?" Still seeing the look, I wondered if I was questioning the wrong guy, a possibility that he had gotten up off the embalming table downstairs and..."Is it raining inside the building?" Finally, "No!"

Just then the real funeral home director arrived on the scene, recognized by the gold pin with his name written on it. So I proceeded with the same deductive logic. "Well, if the water sprinkler system is not working, and there is no smell of smoke, then it has to be a malfunctioning smoke alarm, or maybe time to change the battery?"

"You're so smart!" was his honest, sincere reply, as he patted me on the shoulder. "Thank you! You're right. I never thought of that!" Next, I adventured to ask if the alarm system was wired into the fire department, but at that very moment rescinded the question. . . I heard them coming.

The serenity that the funeral home grounds had provided was instantly destroyed with the arrival of the block-long hook-and-ladder fire truck, three regular fire trucks, two rescue units and six police cars, all arriving in a grand manner, lights a flashing and sirens a blaring, loud enough to wake the dead, and what more appropriate location. . . IF they could locate where that caravan of caskets that went flying down the hall a moment ago had gone.

Into the cathedral chapel flooded a full platoon of combat ready firemen in full gear, axes, and hoses in hand, ready to do battle. This platoon of men who were ready to challenge the elements of the moment was suddenly brought to a halt upon finding me in the center aisle of the chapel in my finest Statue of Liberty pose, pointing up to the smoke alarm located in the very tip-top of the cathedral ceiling. Trust me; it was a proud moment for me, even though it was short lived. I had been a beacon of light for solving one of mankind's greatest problems, "Don't forget to change the batteries in your smoke alarm."

The next two hours reminded me of old black and white movie of the "Three Stooges." with a touch of Abbott and Costello's "Who's on First?" thrown in for good measure. The ladder was first too short, then too tall, and then it wouldn't fit between the pews which had to be removed.

"Who's got a screwdriver?" someone yelled, and the search took the next twenty minutes. But the biggest joke of all was when finally reaching the top of the cathedral ceiling with the tallest fire department's ladder, someone barked from above, "Where're the batteries? Somebody got new batteries?" Watching the mad scramble of funeral home attendants searching for new batteries and blaming each other for not knowing where they were, all I could think of was, thank goodness they work with the dead. They can't talk back!

Forty five minutes later, the battery was replaced, pews screwed back down, and the ladder was removed. Almost two and a half hours from the first sound of the smoke alarm, Hettie Mae's service was about to begin.

All the flowers had been removed from Hettie Mae's visitation room and moved to the chapel and just the casket remained. Walking to the head of the casket, being escorted by my Butler James, the head funeral home director once again made his apologies for the delay and all the inconvenience it may have caused the family. "Reverend, would you lead us in prayer?"

Clearing my throat several times I tried to get everyone's attention, because by now, due to the delay, the funeral had almost turned into a family reunion. "Shall we pray?" I said, repeating myself several more times, producing more volume each time. But bowing my head only signaled another "Preach-ah" from Lula Jane as she pointed one finger in my direction as she and Sister Raymond headed to the nearest restroom for a "re-do" of fresh paint (lipstick) and powdered noses. When would I remember that southern women must keep certain traditions, even at funerals? When some element of quiet was finally obtained, I again bowed my head to pray.

Following the funeral director into the chapel, asking the audience to please stand, we all took our places. Walking past the casket and starting up the platform steps, I was suddenly stopped dead in my tracks. Right in front of my direct eye contact with the family was that tacky Styrofoam arrangement, "Jesus called." There would be no way I could look at the family and the other guests in the eye while trying to overlook this hideous object. Just as the family passed the casket, Lula Jane said loudly enough for all to hear, "I took care of you, Preach-ah. I know how much you loved that arrangement so I had the director put it right here so you could enjoy it."

Finally after a long prayer to help distract my attention from that Styrofoam arrangement and what I was called to do, I read the Scripture.

Regaining my composure, all I wanted to do was take that plastic phone off that hideous arrangement and call up Jesus and simply yell out, "HELP!"

With the service being concluded, we were ushered out into our waiting cars and one hour later we arrived at the grave site. By now the heavens had opened wide and it was pouring rain. Standing under the grave tent I watched the little old ladies put on their plastic rain bonnets, taking small steps while hanging on to their canes and umbrellas on their way to the tent.

It was now pouring so hard that it was coming down in sheets. Under the tent that covered the grave were pockets of water hanging down from the ceiling of the tent, which I knew any moment could give way and come crashing down on everyone, not to mention the demise of the tent itself.

"We are gathered here . . ." began my short grave side service; when I happened to look down to see the casket was covered in plastic, plastic bags from the cleaners. Why was I surprised? Everything in Hettie Mae's home had been covered in plastic for years. She had known no difference.

"This concludes the service . . ." Like a switch had been turned on, the grieving family members suddenly changed gears from grief to family reunion mode, as they hurried back to their cars. There I stood - soaked to the bone - and they were having a great time. It wasn't fair, I thought. The funeral director walked over and lifted the saddle blanket off the casket preparing to lower it into the grave. Then, it hit me! By George, she's not going out with plastic slip covers over her casket!

Before my mind passed my childhood of living in a plastic world. My mother had covered every piece of furniture as well as the carpet with plastic, to be removed only when company came!

Suddenly, without even giving it a second thought, I took hold of the plastic dry cleaner bags from the casket and with one final, fatal jerk, pulled those babies off! Rolling them up and laying them on the ground, I turned and walked out into the rain and toward my car.

Stopping only a few feet from the tent, I looked back over my shoulder to observe the final scene as Hettie Mae's casket was lowered into the ground. Looking up into the heavens, the rain pouring on my face, I couldn't help but think that now she was hearing and enjoying the sounds of heaven and the voice of God for the very first time.

Unable to contain myself, I started laughing out loud. Hettie Mae was now walking streets of gold without a single thing being covered in plastic. Just as her casket was lowered out of sight, there was a gentle clap of thunder, followed by a wisp of wind blowing the rolled up plastic across the cemetery. "You're welcome, Hettie Mae! No more plastic!"

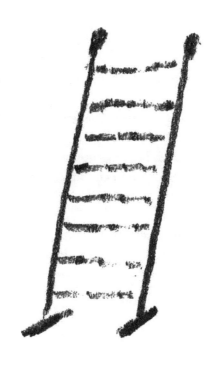

"I Should Have Prayed First"

Ahh . . . serenity, a freshly brewed cup of coffee, its aroma filling my head with thoughts of some distant, uninhabited island. Just me and my cat Tacky, who now avoids the fireplace like the plague, since he caught his tail on fire. These were the moments of solitude I cherished before the rat race of my current life began on a daily basis.

The tranquility of the moment was shattered like the forces of a 9.9 earthquake, knocking Me back into reality, causing me to spill my cup of hot serenity, and sending Tacky, with instant memory recall of a fireplace, running for cover. I instantly recognized the ringing of my phone and didn't have to look to see who was calling. I could tell by the teeth- rattling sound that it was none other than Digger O'Dell, the friendly undertaker (*not his real name, of course, just a fictitious name from the 1950's*). Digger's real name was Lureen Gene! Bless his heart; his mother had to have had issues!

Digger, or should I have said, Lureen Gene, was five by five in stature, bald-headed, and sporting a pencil fine line mustache located below his big nose that always captured one's attention as it moved in and out as he spoke. When he really got nervous or excited, it would move from side to side and then shift into it's up and down mode. His mustache worked as a retaining wall between the end of his nose and his upper lip as he perspired beyond normalcy. His complete baldness could be attributed to his constant wiping his head with his beige colored handkerchief. He had rubbed off all his hair over the years! But that wasn't all; he had a routine you could bet on. Upon leaving his bald head, his handkerchief would quickly move down one side or the other of his face, then around to the back of his neck and ending up wiping his "Adam's Apple." Bless his heart, as he aged he started applying some embalming makeup, the amount depending on how bad his wrinkles looked that morning. He didn't realize what a number that pink light would play on his age spots!

Lureen, I mean Digger O'Dell, the friendly undertaker, in spite of his almost comical stature, seemed to have everything under his control. His friendly funeral home had for years sponsored the livestock market daily noon report on WWZY radio, signing off with appropriate organ music in the background with Digger quoting his favorite corny slogan, "We'll be the last to let you down" following the hog market report. Of course, if there was an upcoming Jewish funeral in the community, he would report on the chicken market, not hogs. So thoughtful of others, bless his heart! All other religions got the smorgasbord of livestock reports. Lately the vegans have totally wiped him off their schedules.

As I said, Digger seemed to have everything under his control, or at least had a monopoly on things, even though he required his customers to transport the casket to the mortuary if purchased from a different business, such as Walmart, (*cheaper, of course*) refusing to make the pickup himself. From owning the primary number one funeral home in town and the leading florist shop next door, to owning the "Wholesale Casket Sales and Rentals", all his bases seemed to be covered. That is, until Walmart moved out on the hard road and started undercutting his prices for caskets. This forced Digger to give a baked ham and coleslaw after the service, enough to feed a family of six, allowing him to keep a competitive edge.

Knowing I should answer the phone, but not wanting to, left me no choice but to answer. I was a single mother of two, and that ring tone meant money. I was the funeral home organist. It wasn't a high paying job that would rocket me into the status of a Rockefeller, but every little bit helped. Not that I'm complaining mind you. I had a roof over my head, enough food to make me fat, and sufficient clothes from Good Will to allow a change every other day. Let's just put it this way. When I went to the grocery store, I could usually go through the fast lane, 15 items or less, since that was the extent of my funds. My friends were completely unaware that I was living life in the "fast lane"! Knowing all of this, I knew the necessity of answering the phone, regardless of how badly I wanted to stay on my uninhabited island and pour myself another cup of coffee.

As I walked toward the ringing phone, my musical life passed through my mind. By the time I was thirteen I was playing the piano at church fairly regularly, and sometimes the organ. So now in my adult years, this was like breathing—no big deal. But when the idea of playing for funerals *(of all things!)* was put into my head, I didn't give it much thought except that it might be a little scary.

But then I was approached by this little old lady at church about doing just that. I thought, well, hey, not much work and a little bit of money to enlarge my coffers! And who could resist the pleading eyes of Miss Mable? After all, she had been in the funeral business for 40 *(or 50? or 60?)* years and had done it all, from arranging the hair of the deceased *(O yuck!)* to greeting the grieving families to make "arrangements". And if Miss Mable thought I could do this, I guess I could! She was retiring, and after enduring several "marginal" organists, she was sure I was just the ticket! So that's how it started, and I soon realized that this was a great deal!

"So answer the phone," I said to myself. "Why the hesitation?" When Digger called it was always a dissertation that lasted for what appeared to be hours. You could lay the phone down, leave the room, do the laundry, walk back, grunt into the phone, lay it back down and go and do something else and not miss any important information he wished to convey. If you weren't dead already, he could talk you to death!

So when I heard his voice, I knew what to expect. In his quiet, funeral voice, (*signifying for sure that the family of the deceased was sharing the room*) he began to speak. "We have a service at 10:00 a.m. on Saturday and the family is wondering if you would be available to play the organ."

After I had answered in the affirmative, he continued, "We would like the selection of music to correlate with the remainder of the service, if that is agreeable with you." I understood that "correlation" was the operative word here. Maybe the next thing they would come up with would be having the same color on everything. Maybe light brown should be the color of the day: light brown funeral hearse, family limo, flowers (*really? Light brown flowers?? And light brown music?*) Although not seen during a service,I might be required to wear, you guessed it, a light brown two piece suit, making us all, cars included, look like a bowl of "gone bad, weak chocolate pudding!" Now I'm really getting carried away!

And so it went. Oh, I'll be there Saturday morning, come snow, wind, or rain, dressed in my two-piece suit but hopefully not light brown!

Anticipating a few extra moments of serenity and quietness that morning at the funeral home, I made my way across town. I had stopped at Marvin's Coffee Mart for my favorite decaf, which was relaxing me as I drove.

Digger's Funeral Home was located on the top of a small hill with a long winding driveway, making its way among the lush manicured lawns with flower gardens, fountains, and waterfalls. The serenity it portrayed was most comforting. It would have made a beautiful wedding chapel if there hadn't been a big sign at the front of the hill proclaiming loud and clear, "Digger's Memorial Chapel!"

I was almost to the top of the hill when I was suddenly overcome with chills up my spine, quickly looking at my watch, thinking I was late. I never saw so many police cars and SUVs in all my life, marked and unmarked, black in nature with tinted windows. Standing around the grounds were men in black suits, wearing dark sunglasses, speaking into their wrists, with ear cords attached to their ears. Their eyes were like giant animals, darting every which direction, and stalking their prey. (*Hey, I recognize these big black SUVs as the FEDs when I see them! My TV time hasn't been totally wasted!*)

Suddenly I screamed bloody-murder as one of these "G-I-Joes" stepped out of nowhere and into the path of my old Buick, causing me to instantly slam on my brakes. This sent him into orbit as he slid across the hood of my car, ending up against my windshield like a squashed June bug. The windshield wipers and washers, now activated, began spraying him in such a manner that one might think he had lost control of some, if not all, of his bodily functions.

Realizing my planned serenity for the day was not actually coming to pass, my mind suddenly jumped into gear. If he had only looked both ways before venturing into the road, all this could have been avoided! Are we talking street manners 101 here?

But now look where we were. My coffee was soaking into my beige suit and his suit looked like a total disaster.

Again, as my teeth were grinding and my blood pressure was ascending, (*Maybe that decaf wasn't!*) I wanted to yell a few cute phrases I never get to use, but I didn't. After all, this was a FED, and I wasn't about to end up in Leavenworth, or wherever they put folks like me who talk back to the FEDS! I couldn't help wondering how my outspoken mother would have handled this situation. I'm sure she would have given them a "what for" while asking a bunch of questions such as what they were doing there in the first place and why in the world where they wearing those stupid sunglasses so we couldn't see their faces.

Before he had time to take the sunglasses off, my car was surrounded by more of them wearing the same dark sunglasses, dark suits and talking into their wrists. All I could think of was that there must have been a sale on black suits, dark sunglasses, and wrist telephones.

Without questioning me, they pulled my door open and I

found myself standing next to my car with my hands on top of my old Buick. So much for a quiet morning of serenity.

Not to my surprise, none of them were paying attention as I was trying to explain who I was as they kept going through my car, looking for something. Just then, flying out of the front door of the funeral home, was my rescuer, Digger O'Dell.

"She's all right! She works for me! She's my organist!" he yelled, almost rolling over to where I stood. He began wiping his bald head with his beige handkerchief. . . You guessed it: down the side of his face, to the back of his neck, and ending up on his Adam's Apple.

Stepping out from among the group of men dressed in black, their apparent leader said, "OK, men! Let her go!" And with the warmth of a marble statue, (*or with the warmth of a six day old corpse*), he sputtered, "Sorry, Ma'am."

Digger quickly ushered me into the funeral home and into his office. "I'm sorry about what's just happened to you. I just got word this morning that the FBI would be involved in this service. Are you all right?"

As usual, a man thing, ignoring me, thinking only of business, he continued, "I can't figure out just yet if this is gonna be a good advertisement or a bad one once the newspaper gets a hold of it. Anyway, the grandson of the deceased is being allowed to leave prison to attend his grandmother's funeral service. I don't know who he is but I've heard that he's some guy involved in the mob. I can't remember exactly what they call him. These men in the black suits sure won't tell me a thing but this guy must have been involved in a federal crime or they wouldn't be here. They're taking no chances he might try to escape or, God forbid, somebody taking him out! Oh, and another thing. When you get to the organ room and look out at the mourners, you'll see a few uniformed police. That's just in case any ...ah...ah... disturbance breaks out up by the casket. There...ah... ah...has been a history of disturbances with this particular family."

Oh! That's comforting to know! I thought to myself. This time, airing my thoughts, I asked, "And when do I get hazardous pay?"

"We'll see," Digger replied. Quietly I uttered my response. "Well, I do have the last word, you understand. I could be real "creative" in what I play at this service. How 'bout "Happy Days Are Here Again," as they wheel Granny in? You want advertisement or hazardous pay? Your choice!" Well, where did that come from? That sure didn't sound like quiet, genteel, me!

I made my way back to the organ room, my knees knocking a tune of their own, my mind racing a mile a minute. What in the world was I going to play for a convict's grandma's funeral? What are suitable hymns, knowing there would be a criminal seated a few feet from me. "God Will Take Care of You"? or "I Need Thee Every Hour"? "Till the Storm Passes By"?

I wondered what this particular service might be like since the preliminaries had been one for the books. My mind began to imagine all kinds of things happening. Do I plan an escape route, or call my kids and tell them good-bye? Should I ask for police protection since they were here anyway?

I had always been glad that I could see and not be seen as I sat in the organ room on my "perch". Today I was thinking I didn't want to see OR be seen! Not knowing many details of why the police were there, I began to hallucinate about the situation. (*I would learn later why the preponderance of police presence. The young prisoner's parents were divorced and each side blamed the other for the way the boy had turned out. One side didn't even want him at the service, had totally turned against him. The other thought it only fair that he attend his grandmother's funeral. So, because of past calls of domestic disturbance, actually violence, the police had been called in to protect the innocent, that being poor Granny's remains. Should a fight break out near the casket, well, you know the rest.*) Did they have guns with them? Surely they wouldn't come here without being fully armed! Did they know how to fire them successfully, or would wild shooting occur and bullets would be blazing in every direction, especially mine?

I had only been joking with Digger when I said I would play "Happy Days Are Here Again" when Granny's casket was wheeled into the chapel, but now I began to think of something more like, "The Fight is On", or one for myself, "Flee as a Bird"! But I couldn't help thinking an Elvis rendition of "Jailhouse Rock" would be more than appropriate!

Well, between spilled coffee, a lack of serenity, and enough law enforcement to police the western hemisphere, so far so good. No fights loud enough to wake up Granny had broken out, and the FBI dudes had settled in with renewed hopes of a short uneventful service, eyes on the convict, hands on holsters. Me? I just wanted to get this show on the road, and I had to admit that "uneventful" wasn't even in my vocabulary at this point. Too much had already happened! Let's just forget this "decaf" thing and get me a triple latte. Does Marvin's Coffee Mart deliver?

What I needed was a distraction, something to keep my mind from disintegrating into a cesspool of "what if's". It didn't take long and the distraction came in the form of a little old lady who shuffled into the organ room, unannounced, and introduced herself.

"Excuse me," she said in mousy tones! "Are you the organist?" I wanted to say, "No, I'm just sitting her, dusting the bench off. The cleaning lady couldn't make it today!" But I didn't! I knew I would have to ask God for forgiveness for my attitude on this one. She couldn't help it if those dark suit characters outside had spoiled my day and spilled my decaf!

She couldn't be more than 4 feet 7, I thought as I stared at this little old lady with shades of purple and blue hair. I knew she either had done a "home job" of putting a rinse on her hair, had it done at a beauty salon, and obviously paid way too much money, or worse yet, came through the embalming room and Digger had practiced on her. Regardless, she was dressed in purple, tasteful for a funeral, big pearls hanging gracefully around her fragile little neck. Her outfit was completed by the white gloves she wore. She obviously knew that no true southern lady would attend a funeral without her white gloves. They weren't for fashion purposes only, for they covered the age and liver spots on her hands, stopping her relatives from judging how old she really was and wondering if she would be next to "check out!" Layers of makeup and a big hat casting shadows across her face took care of the guessers as well as the wrinkles.

As our conversation continued, I was informed that she hadn't sung in public since first grade, and that she didn't read a note of music, causing my stomach to do a flip. She didn't have any music, but did I know "Amazing Grace," and "The Old Rugged Cross"? My stomach now flipped again. Right about now I was praying for some of that "Amazing Grace!"

I drew a big breath, wanting to ask God, "Why me?", but chose rather to smile and say, "That's okay. I have music to those two songs and you're welcome to use it, if needs be."

Normally we have four regular singers who work for the funeral home, who know the ropes and what needs to be sung, where to stand, making it a breeze for the organist. But then, there is on occasion, like now, where they refuse to use the funeral home singers and bring in one of their relatives to sing. That's when anything can happen and usually does! But don't worry. There are plenty of relatives to praise them for the wonderful job they had done!

Playing the introduction to "Amazing Grace" I waited for the soloist to come in, but there was no singing, plus she was nowhere in sight. Peering over the top of the organ trying to find her, I spied our little elderly guest, compact in hand, applying another layer of powder and bright ruby red lipstick. I slowly repeated the introduction waiting for her to put things away, and I should have waited even longer, for when she finally did start singing, she was singing in one key, I was playing in another. I quickly tried to match her key, but every time I thought I had figured it out, she changed keys herself. I tried everything to get this poor little old lady back on pitch from playing with just one finger to playing just the foot pedals. I was desperate with this lady, but more so every time my mind drifted to what could happen in this crazy service in just a few short minutes.

I never thought I would encounter this, but one of my wrist-talking "Barneys," from Mayberry, arrived telling us that everyone had to clear the funeral home as they were "sweeping" the building and that all guests would be waiting outside for permission to re-enter.

After the "sweep" of the building, as they called it, was over, another unexpected guest arrived. It was none other than the FBI man who had stepped in front of my moving car.

"What are you doing back here?" I asked wondering if I was in trouble with the FEDs again.

"Well, you know what my suit looks like after our unfortunate...a...accident, so they wanted me out of sight for the time being."

Just then Digger came in and instructed me that the service wasn't ready to start just yet, that our special guest from the state prison hadn't arrived, and he had his orders to wait. "After you start playing, just continue till he gets here," he said. Spotting the FBI gentleman seated in the corner was enough to make him leave abruptly.

I had to chuckle to myself at the irony of it all, yet spotting G-I-Joe's gun attached to his hip brought it all back into perspective. Silence filled the room as neither one of us spoke. Suddenly I was aware of quizzical eyes upon me. Turning slightly, I could see my unwanted guest watching me.

"Is there a problem here?' I softly questioned.

"Sorry! I didn't mean to stare, but I'm amazed at all those buttons and keys and pedals you have to know about. I could never get used to all that!"

"I couldn't do what you do either, jumping in front of cars for a living!" sliding that little remark in between our unwanted conversation.

"Touché!" was followed by a short pause, "I'm an FBI agent . . ." and the conversation was on. "How long have you been playing the organ in the funeral business? Doesn't it get depressing? Make you want to cry?" One question after another seemed to be spilling out from his curious mind.

One thing led to an exchange of funny things that happened

in the funeral business, as I explained that if you don't laugh you'll cry because of the nature of the work. I explained that I never really intended to be disrespectful of those listening to my music, but nevertheless I was always glad no one could read my mind as I tickled the ivories.

"I understand. I know how I feel when we have to take someone down. But tell me more!" he said, acting like a little child not wanting to go to bed, wanting more of the story.

"Here in my little room I get a view of the fashion attire some people wear to funerals nowadays. Hole-y jeans with beer T-shirts are the worst! Or hats! Not many wear them these days but when they do, look out! We had a lady last week, seated right there in the second row wearing this outlandish hat. There was no way on God's green earth anyone seated behind her could see anything but her hat. Then my mind began to wander: Wonder what that thing cost? Probably won the lottery...or used her entire monthly food allowance to get that one!"

"Or the screaming child seated in the front row! O I hate that! The louder I play, the louder he cries. I know the parents are embarrassed, but why don't they just take him out?" (*Well, take him out of the room. Not "take him out" as in FBI jargon!*)

"Don't you wonder why some funerals are so small? Did the deceased not have many friends or associates—even acquaintances? Or may......be he failed the course on "How to Win Friends and Influence People". Of course, a logical explanation is that he outlived all his friends! How sad is that?"

The FBI dude sadly shook his head but continued questioning me with, "Ever selected the wrong piece of music for a service and realized it halfway through the song?"

"Have I ever! It was a nightmare! Not so much of me picking the wrong song, but the family wanting the wrong song played, in my opinion. I was stuck in traffic one day, got to the funeral home just in time as Digger handed me an order of service. 'Nothing different, same old songs, you know them all. You've played them for years. Just wing it.'"

"Not paying attention, the service went according to plan. My mistake was that I had not read ahead. I had heard that the deceased had committed suicide by jumping off a bridge into the Illinois River so you can understand my horror that the family had requested that the congregation stand and sing the old hymn, "Shall We Gather at the River" as the casket was being pushed up the center aisle. I just dismissed it from my mind with, 'I just work here. What would I know?' What could I have done anyway?"

"I know I've made a lot of mistakes in my life, but one sticks out in my mind as a real doozie! I was in a big hurry one day—what else is new?—and when I went in to play the organ for a service, I forgot to turn off my cell phone. The soloist was singing the final song, 'Softly and Tenderly Jesus is Calling' when my cell phone rang—not so softly and definitely not tenderly! And to top it off, my ring tone was Reveille! Had the lady in the casket sat straight up, I'd have been asked, "And where would you like your new door?"

The FBI dude just smiled and shook his head as if in disbelief.

Turning the pages of my hymnal, trying to find music more fitting for this special occasion, I continued. "Sometimes I even find myself judging the deceased!"

"You do?" His question flew at me like a bullet from his gun!

"Yes!" I quickly responded. "Especially if the deceased was someone I didn't know. By listening to the minister and what he has to say, I can sometimes tell where the individual went, heaven or hell. Of course this isn't always possible, since every person lying in a casket has somehow lived an exemplary life, full of good deeds and happy experiences, according to many preachers. Or, maybe the deceased was murdered, and everyone thought it was an accident. Let's see . . . that widow looks like her grief could be a LITTLE bit fake"

"Whoa!" I suddenly stopped in midstream. "I must have been watching too many Perry Mason reruns!"

"Speaking of mysteries, sometimes one of the soloists has a habit of arriving just a minute or two before a service. Usually, that is okay because he is a seasoned performer, but from time to time

I wonder if I will have to double as organist AND soloist! He's fine with his late arrivals but I think I've added some gray hair each time he's almost late!" It was time for our FBI agent to chime in.

"In other words, if the soloist or the preacher is late, or like now, the special guest hasn't arrived, you must 'fill in'. Or, sad to say, when the family has a hard time saying good-bye to their loved one, you must play on. Right?"

Quickly interrupting, I said, "Well, Superwoman I'm not! But you're right!

"In other words," my FBI guest continued, "you say the organist isn't the 'star performer' but does provide the 'glue' that holds things together?"

"I guess someone needs to tell that to Digger. Maybe he hasn't figured out that the funeral home organist is like the mailman— through snow, rain, hail, or dark of night—she keeps her funeral commitment! How's that for asking for respect?" I openly inquired.

Looking at his watch, he responded, "I wonder what's keeping the state troopers with their delivery?" Drawing a big sigh, he sat back down. "Any more stories of what has happened on your watch?" he asked with eager mind.

"Well, there was the time Digger called and asked if I could play a funeral on Sunday afternoon. "Digger!" I sputtered, knowing how much I needed the money. "That's right during the Chief's football game!" 'Not to worry,' Digger replied. 'I'll bring a TV and you can watch the game during the funeral.'

"Did he?" eagerly questioned my FBI dude.

"Right on cue, when I showed up that Sunday afternoon, there was the TV! Fortunately neither the organ or the TV were visible to the audience."

"This funeral home boss of yours has quite a sense of humor," added FBI dude.

"I wouldn't go that far. Stubborn man that he is, he refused to let me turn up the sound!

"Speaking of the devil," I said, as Digger entered the room carrying my large Marvin's coffee.

Taking a huge drink of my delicious decaf, I continued, charged with renewed energy. "I remember a Jewish man whose service was totally Catholic. His widow was a devoted Catholic, and you guessed it, she sent his Jewish relatives over the edge. I always felt bad for the poor man. But I guess he was beyond caring at this point, probably fully aware that his wife always got her way anyway, and there was no point in fighting it!"

"Oh, at another Catholic service I played for, all the mourners came into the church quietly and sat in the back rows. When the priest came in, he mentioned that they were obviously good Catholics since they were sitting in the back. (*Silly me! I thought it was only Baptists who did that!*) He then requested they come to the front, which they did."

"Obviously, each funeral is different, has its own unique 'flavor,'" I continued, "but as I look back, many just seem to 'run together' while a few are steeped in my mind for eternity.'"

"How about one more story 'for the road'?" questioned my visitor.

"One more story? Well, I must tell you, Mr. FBI agent, this organist is the complete version of the stereotypical female, 'standing on chair, holding up skirt, screaming furiously' at the sight of a mouse, no matter how infinitesimal!

One day I was to play a funeral in a small but quaint chapel in the cemetery. The organ was small but adequate, the pedals being few and the floor could be plainly seen under them. It was a cold January day with the ground covered with snow. After warming up a bit, I put my heavy coat on the sofa nearby and shed my boots for my organ shoes. As I was playing and folks were coming in, I suddenly spied a mouse running across the floor heading straight toward me! No, I didn't scream, but I considered it! But what exactly would I do if he did go under the organ? If that happened, believe me there would be no more bass pedals played that day!

Anyway, after playing the prelude, the mouse seemed to have disappeared and the service progressed without incident. Even though the funeral had ended, my mind was still occupied with that little critter, so much so that when I picked up my boots; I shook them vigorously, fearing his second appearance. Nothing. Hugely relieved, I put on my boots and picked up my coat. But alas! That little intruder hadn't passed me by after all, but instead had decided to jump out of his warm hiding place in my coat and scare the wits out of me! As I look back on that day, I think if those mouse issues didn't get resolved, my little mouse's great, great, great, great, great grandchildren are reigning to this day!"

Responding, he said, "Remind me not to go to that chapel! I'm not so fond of mice myself!"

Just then, Digger re-entered the room and announced that the special guest had arrived. Looking through my viewing curtains, I scanned the center aisle of the chapel just in time to see our special guest. Wearing a bullet-proof vest, handcuffs, leg irons, and a chain around his waist, he was attached to another officer, and flanked by FBI agents, dark sunglasses and all! My FBI agent quickly snapped into action, his friendly demeanor suddenly changing. He whispered to me, "Thanks for the enlightening and informative conversation. "YOU CAN'T MAKE THIS STUFF UP, REALLY!" Little did he know how much I wanted to play 'Happy Days Are Here Again" at that moment. He was back in his "FBI comfort zone" and we could start the service!*

*This chapter is a compilation of several funerals, people, and events—with enhancement in transition to protect the living and the dead.

Potpourri

DISCLAIMER: This chapter with its collection of potpourri items was never meant to be a politically correct piece of literature. Nor was it meant to please those who are attempting to establish the morals of society in today's climate. Chapter 11 is just the messenger presenting a collection of the far side of human nature that appears at times to have been lost in trying to be politically correct at the expense of others. This collection of potpourri items has been in the process of being collected since humans were able to laugh at themselves and others without being condemned.

All names, locations, and unknown sources have been removed to protect those both living and dead. To those who have contributed we say, "thank you" for your input since we have long forgotten your name and sources.

So if you've advanced this far in reading this book, then you must be part of those forgotten generations who know how to laugh at themselves and at others. Enjoy human nature at some of its finest moments.

Part 1- Funeral Etiquette:

Funerals aren't funny, but sometimes funny things happen and are said to be proof to the medical community that there is a disease called "Hoof-in-Mouth" Syndrome. Doctors know what causes it. It happens when the brain wasn't put in gear and the mouth slipped the clutch, stripping the gears and causing one to say the wrong thing at the wrong time. At the present, there is no cure for those afflicted with said disease, short of removing the tongue.

Probably topping the list of "wrong thing at the wrong time" are condolences expressed to the bereaved. Many of us feel uncomfortable at the visitation or funeral because we don't know what to say. Having officiated at scores of funerals, I've acquired a listing of what NOT to say to the grieving. Having had experience with those suffering from "Hoof-in-mouth" Syndrome, I must say some of their attempts to console are downright hilarious, some blunt, while others only bring on, "You've got to be kidding me! They really didn't say that . . . did they?" The answer is a simple "yes". But not to worry! None of these will be a candidate for the Nobel Prize—for peace or anything else! So here goes!

What NOT to say:

- Boy! You wouldn't believe the day I'm having when approaching the grieving party
- Do you validate parking?
- Can we pick up this visitation thing? I've got Jazzercise at four.
- Whoa! I didn't know we were supposed to dress up!
- Hey! Let's order pizza!
- I'd have gotten a second opinion if I had been you!
- Is there Karaoke afterwards? The organist wants to know.
- He won't be needing that tie anymore after the service, will he?
- Isn't that the same jacket he wore to the junior prom when we were in high school?
- Hey, can we take the funeral procession through the Taco Bell drive-through?

- Finally! I can get a picture of him with his mouth shut. Say cheese!
- Oh my goodness, you mean this isn't the Scientology seminar?
- It's about time he quit smoking!
- Is that his real hair?
- Did anybody check his pockets for coupons?
- Stick a fork in him . . . he's done!
- I share your grief. My iguana died this morning. You've got my sympathy!
- Count your blessings. You didn't lose much.
- Was he cheating on you?
- Now, are you the wife or the girlfriend? You two look so much alike!
- Did he donate all his organs to science? I thought so. This coffin is really light.
- I know this is probably a bad time but . . . just before your husband fell to his death . . . did he happen to mention anything about that drill he borrowed?
- I wouldn't be caught dead in that outfit! (*Don't be so catty! Maybe the widower picked out her clothing. Death is not a style show!*)
- Are you videotaping the service? I might have to leave early.
- I know it's a closed casket service, but just a little peek-a-doodle?
- I'd give this funeral . . . say on a scale of one to ten . . . possibly a six.
- I hope they did an autopsy on him . . . something smells fishy if you ask me!
- I declare, she looks better than she ever did!
- You plan on having a yard sale next week with your wife's things?
- You're not going to believe how much I had to fork out for the funeral spray. I brought the bill in case you didn't believe me.

- Don't take this personally, friend, but this is the smallest funeral I've ever seen. You should have called me, I'd have put some glitz into it!
- Hey, you need me to make a beer run?
- I hate to tell you, but there's a man from the IRS who wants to see you in the funeral home office.
- Have any of the flowers been spoken for after the service? I'd like to take mine home instead of letting them die out at the cemetery.
- How soon you puttin' Fred's Cadillac up for sale? What are you askin' for it?
- Since Fred was a retired military man, do you mind if I play "Taps" on my kazoo at the grave site?
- Just to relieve your mind, we're taking up a collection to help pay his gambling debts.
- Are you on any medication? If not, I've got a purse full. You name it, I've got it!
- I've got a heavy-duty disease and I need my medicine, but I had to come and say how sorry I was. (*It's not about you on this day. Your turn to die is in your future!*)
- Child, I haven't seen you in a long time . . . Isn't it just awful? So sudden! But remember, she's "asleep in Gee-sus". (*Save your Lady Macbeth performance for the stage. Your shallow emotional outburst is not appreciated by the grieving relatives.*)
- She looks like she's asleep! (*When was the last time you were in her bedroom watching her sleep??*)

OTHER ETIQUETTE TIPS

- Some survivors will have the funeral home arrange the floral pieces before the guests start arriving. Remember that the larger the piece (*or the larger the influence of the giver*), the closer to the family pieces it goes. If you sent a "cheap" floral arrangement, don't swap cards when no one is looking. You are bound to get caught.

– Don't get your feelings hurt if you sent a "peace lily" and it is not appreciated. First of all, peace lilies say either, "Oh, I forgot to send something," or "I forgot you died," or "Well, I've got to send something!" So when you arrive at the visitation, don't be too surprised to find your peace lily across the room on some end table, or resting comfortably out of sight on the floor.

– The horror of horrors, don't go to Publix or Kroger's and buy a $2.95 potted plant of stinky mums, take them to the funeral home yourself, and then expect praises from the bereaved as if you were the King or Queen of England and you graced their presence with the crown jewels!

– If there happens to be a large bowl filled with funeral home matches on the hall table, don't load up! It's tacky! They're too short to light your grill and they bend in the middle anyway.

– This same principle applies if there is a dish of small individually wrapped soaps in the restrooms. If you gotta steal, I guess its okay to take (*steal*) from the Holiday Inn, but not a funeral home. I sure wouldn't want that on my conscience, knowing I was facing my Maker with stolen funeral home soaps in my pocket. Actually, anything from the Holiday Inn applies as well.

HERE IS AN ADDITIONAL LIST OF "DON'TS"

– race the hearse to the cemetery
– sit in the front row of the church and lean over the seat to wave at everyone you know, even if you haven't seen them since the last funeral.

- remark that the deceased looks "way better than he ever did"
- charge for any help you give
- tell the grieving family, "It could have been worse" and then go into a long rambling story about the passing of your dog Blue
- approach the widow/widower and ask for the fifty dollars the deceased owed you
- climb on the headstones to get a better view.
- ask about the "eats" the minute you arrive at the funeral home.
- tell the undertaker that he can't close the coffin until you find your contact lens.
- ask the widow if you can have the body to practice tattooing on.
- ask someone to take a photo of you shaking hands with the deceased
- urge the widow to give the deceased's wooden leg to someone too poor to afford firewood.
- drive behind the widow's limo and keep honking your horn.
- tell the undertaker that your dog just died and ask if you can sneak him into the coffin.
- promise the minister a hundred dollars if he can keep a straight face while praising the deceased.
- try to make the grieving family feel better by handing them a typewritten list of the deceased's faults.
- remove anything from the coffin for a "memento".
- tell everyone you're from the IRS and you're confiscating the coffin for back taxes.
- shout "You've got to be kidding me!" during the eulogy. (*Or any selected expletives, no matter how tempting!*)
- use the word "rooked" if a discussion of funeral expenses arises.

- attend the funeral of someone you don't know. Tacky! Get a life!
- work the crowd, or "schmooze" with a pocketful of business cards. (*No business cards on windshields either!*)
- As to funeral attire, times and customs have radically changed. Blue jeans? Perfectly fine, EXCEPT in our beloved south. Women there had better pull out their expensive (*or not*) hats! Yes, hats! Nobody can make an "entrance" at a funeral like a genteel southern woman. AND, it offers a grand opportunity to display her many grieving talents accented by her drop-dead (*no pun intended*) gorgeous hat! It is against her principles to steal attention away from the grieving widow; she just does! Big hats are not a necessity, but they do serve a purpose, that of drawing attention away from the pain and suffering of the bereaved. If there is a slight smirk, or a gentle gasp coming from the audience, the hat has been successful.
- Many senior citizens are quite confused about how they should dress for a funeral. Feeling young, they try to conform to current fashions, wanting to present a youthful image and not call attention to their aging appearances. Here is a list of items which should NEVER be combined:
- A nose ring and bifocals
- Spiked hair and bald spots
- A pierced tongue and dentures
- Miniskirts and support hose
- Miniskirts and varicose veins
- Ankle bracelets and corn pads
- Speedo's and cellulite
- A belly button ring and a gall bladder scar
- Bikinis and liver spots
- And at some point, the DAISY DUKE SHORTS must remain at home!
- Any more suggestions?

Part 2 - VIGNETTES SMALL AND TALL

Can we insert some READER'S DIGEST-type stories?

— Someone told of a lady who had spent her whole life planning her funeral. She wanted to wear her pink dress for the visitation and her red one for the funeral. A friend tried to talk her out of it but she insisted. "Anyone who knows me knows I wouldn't wear the same dress two days in a row!"

— The story has been told of a little old lady who would attend multiple funerals on a daily basis. After all, who could pass up that potluck dinner at the church? When it came time to close the casket, she would throw herself across the deceased and as the "tears" fell, she would quickly remove any jewelry she could find on the body. In fact, she became so adept at this theft that she became known as a very thoughtful woman, giving expensive gifts to her family and friends at Christmas. She was noted for her taste in fine jewelry. Finally, her family became suspicious and began patting her down like airport security after each day of her "funeral runs." That was the end of expensive gifts at Christmas!

— A man had placed flowers on his mother's grave when his attention was diverted to another man kneeling at a grave. The man seemed to be praying with profound intensity as he kept repeating, "Why did you have to die? Why did you have to die?" The first man approached him and said, "Sir, I don't wish to interfere with your private grief, but this demonstration of pain is more than I've ever seen before. For whom do you mourn so deeply? A child? A parent?" The mourner took a moment to collect himself, then replied.........."My wife's first husband."

– One day a saleswoman promoting a certain brand of brushes knocked on the door and asked the man of the house if she could see his wife. Told that she wasn't home, the saleswoman inquired if she could wait for her. After a three hour wait, she became worried and called out to the man, "May I know where your wife is?" The man of few words replied, "She went to the cemetery."

"And when is she coming home?"

"I really don't know. She's been there eleven years now." The three-hour wait ended!

– The story is told of a kind grocery store owner many years ago. Poverty was everywhere and many of the children were near starvation. Sometimes three little boys would visit his store, explaining they were only "admiring" the food since they had no money. He would ask if they had anything they could "trade" for food. When a marble was produced, the storekeeper would take it and give the boy a sack of food, telling him he really wanted a red marble rather than the blue one. So the boy would take the sack of groceries and come back the next day with the red marble. Then the process was repeated with a different color marble and more groceries taken to the poor home.

When the man died many years later, and the young boys had grown up, the wife took the young men to the casket. She then held up her husband's hand to reveal three red marbles. His legacy lives on!

– Watch out for those cremations! One man went to throw the ashes of his departed father into the ocean when a strong gust of wind hit, blowing his father's ashes back onto him, covering his suit. Every year now on the anniversary of his father's death, he goes and hangs a wreath on the door of his neighborhood cleaners. The only problem, people think the man running the cleaners sure loses a lot of loved ones!

- In a similar case, a family kept the departed in the laundry room next to the Tide, and over a period of time, they wondered why their whites kept getting darker and darker. Their weird aunt who lived with them and had some "loose shingles" was in charge of doing the laundry. Now every year at the anniversary of the death of their loved one, they go down to the sanitation treatment plant and lay flowers on top of one of the ponds.

- On the death of his brother, one man found it necessary to alert the funeral home crematory division that a problem could be looming. The brother had been drunk for years and there was a concern that if he were cremated, it was possible that the whole funeral home might blow up! (*It never happened, but it's good to be warned!*)

- A funeral director was talking on the phone to a grieving widow. "I realize we all grieve in our own way, Ma'am, but the crematorium staff did not appreciate the fireworks you put in your husband's pockets."

- One man planned to bring the ashes of his beloved wife to his mountain cabin, scatter them nearby, and fondly remember her each time he stepped off his front porch. However, the county had determined this would be the time to bring in the heavy equipment to prepare for a new road in front of his cabin. His only choice was to rent a cordless vacuum and vacuum up—you guessed it—the wife's ashes!

- Following a car accident, a critically injured man, now on life support, was verbally assaulted by his very pregnant wife. "Ro............bert!" she screamed. "FINALLY you are going to donate something! I have been donating my time, money, energy, etc. etc. etc. all these years and you never gave ANYTHING TO ANYBODY! Now you'll be donating your heart, your lungs, your kidneys, your liver . . . Oh, not that. Who would want your alcoholic liver?" And she stormed out of the room in a huff, never to return!

– (*This story appeared in a local newspaper.*) There was a wealthy man who in his later life, was cared for by a couple who wanted nothing more than to be of help to him. His son and daughter, however, wanted nothing to do with his care. In fact, the son, during his rare visits to his father, would steal things of value which could be sold. When the man died, the son and daughter were called to view the man's body before it was taken to the mortuary. When the son walked in, he immediately asked, "When do we read the will?" When the will was read, it was discovered that all the son had inherited was all the things he had stolen! The father had kept a record of every one!

– One man's casket was placed in the back of his pickup truck, which had been his "pride and joy". His widow and his nephew rode up front and his two daughters and grandchildren rode in the back on either side of the casket, smiling and waving at anybody and everybody on the way to the cemetery. They busied themselves taking "selfies" of themselves leaning on the casket, making faces, laughing, joking, and later placed these on Facebook.

– A telemarketer made a call, reaching a little old lady. After some small talk, he asked, "Is the mister in the house?" She replied, "He doesn't live here anymore," to which the telemarketer said, "Do you happen to have his new number?" The lady read off the new number, for which he was grateful. After hanging up, he dialed the new number only to get an answering machine saying, "Thank you for calling Green Acres Cemetery."

- A local funeral home sent out a 6X9 mass mailing invitation to attend a seminar on making one's final funeral arrangements, complimentary meal included. On the cover of the mailer was a nice big juicy bacon cheeseburger in glorious color. The funeral home proudly displays the word "Dignity" in any advertisement, so can you explain how a cheeseburger and Dignity go together? Or, can you imagine trying to enjoy a cheeseburger while listening to plans to put you away? Go figure!

- A widow had a bad back and couldn't stand very long next to her husband's casket while receiving guests. Her solution was to lie down on the floor next to the casket and reach up to shake hands with those offering condolences.

- People sometimes place strange things in the caskets of their loved ones; golf clubs, decks of cards, bottles of liquor. One lady placed a can opener in her deceased husband's hand, just in case he needed to get out.

- One family had a sheet cake made in the shape and size of the deceased and served it at the reception following the funeral service.

- At the conclusion of Grandma's funeral service, just before the casket was closed, the large family gathered around the casket for one more family photo while one of the small children held up a sign that said "RIP".

- Another family, husband, wife and two children, insisted on having a family photo taken with the deceased. Reason? They always had a photo taken with Grandpa on special occasions, weddings, reunions, Christmas, and thought this photo would not only be a keepsake but great for this year's Christmas cards.

- To save money, one family decided a hearse to take the casket to the cemetery was unnecessary and decided to do the job themselves. They placed their loved one's casket in the back seat, hanging out the end of the Volkswagen convertible. Caused a few heads to turn on the interstate!

- Thinking of going into the funeral business? Be sure and check out the web site which offers "36 Ideas to Breathe Life Into Your Funeral Home Business".

PART 3 – "THE WORST"

- **Worst Funeral Guests:**
  It goes without saying that engraved invitations won't be sent out to your funeral unless, of course, you alert your printer as to the time and place of your death prior to your cashing things in. Not probable. However, if you were going to send out your own invitations, there might be a few people you would want to eliminate from your list. Consider the following:

- "All My Ex's Live in Texas" may not be the case for most people but you might want to think twice about letting someone invite your "ex's" to your funeral. Could be they would make a fuss over just about anything . . . telling folks they deserve to be in the will, demanding to sit with the current wife/husband, or worse yet, demanding to know why they weren't given a plot next to the deceased's, even though they were spouse #three twice removed.

- Then there's the long-lost relative who might show up for the service (*uninvited, of course, but unstoppable as well!*) Hardly anyone recognizes him since he hasn't been seen since several funerals back. (*Could it be that the reading of the will has brought him out of the woodwork?*) He struts in wearing his typical Floridian attire: canvas tennis shoes, light blue double knit slacks, and a short-sleeved shirt covered in pink flamingos, buttons stretched to their limits over his beer belly. Fortunately, he has discarded his half-chewed cigar on entering the room. He wants everyone to know how "brilliant" in Bible knowledge he is and works the room prior to the service asking who knows what the shortest verse in the Bible would be. Obviously, it's the only verse he ever bothered to memorize. "Jesus Wept" just rolls off his tongue!

– All those who love sickness and death more than life seem to gravitate to funerals. They LOVE exchanging funeral and colonoscopy stories. It always ends with an argument as to who has the biggest and most polyps. Someone finally put an end to said argument by suggesting they take pictures of their next colonoscopy and put them on their Christmas cards. Poor Aunt Clara, who is deaf, bless her heart, thought it was a wonderful idea and said she'd order two boxes.

– And we wouldn't want to forget Uncle Buford! He always shows up at family reunions and funerals looking for his next bride. Success hasn't been his friend in this arena, but his motto continues to be, "Hope springs eternal!" He worries everyone, especially at family funerals, with his loose-fitting dentures, since stories about his losing them at inopportune times continue to circulate. (*Such as in the casket, punch bowl, etc.*) Aunt Mable, who has fainted numerous times due to Uncle Buford's fast-flying dentures, says her heart wouldn't survive another such episode.

Worst Funeral Home Names:

– Butcher Funeral Home
– Ronald McDonald II Funeral Home

- Cease Funeral Home
- Burns Funeral Home and Crematory
- Hollerbach Funeral Home
- Stabb Polk Memorial Home
- Dye Funeral Home
- Moody Funeral Home and Chapel
- Cook Funeral Home and Crematory
- Baloney Funeral Home
- Leavitt Funeral Home
- Bruce and Stiff Funeral Home
- Downer Funeral Home
- Ratterman Funeral Home (This name was on a large sign with other firms. Under the funeral home name was "Clown School" starts in October. Call Ruth.)
- Toon Funeral Home (*Next to a parking lot sign - "exit only"*)
- Bury Funeral Home
- Bizzardo Funeral Home
- Young's Funeral Home and Crematory. This was an electronic sign. Young Funeral Home was at the top, and it's name never changed, but the listing of the firms below the funeral home's name changed. The first one under the funeral home was
- "Contagious"; when it changed it read, "Free Breakfast".
- The third one was, "Awww... Pete just died, but free pancakes, Whoo Hoo!)
- Guido Funeral Home (*I guess this is one the Mob used*)
- Slaughter and Sons Funeral Home

WORST FUNERAL HOME SLOGANS:

- <u>WORST "OUT FRONT" SLOGANS</u> " (For real!)
- If they're dead, they're here!
- 50% off your next funeral
- Please come again!

- You wouldn't want to be seen dead with anyone else!
- Why walk around half dead? We will bury you for $199.99, plus we give Green Stamps.
- Group rates available!
- Call before you dig. (*Bumper sticker on the back of a hearse.*)
- Our guests are dying to meet you.
- We must be good, people are dying to get in.
- Drive carefully. We'll wait.
- Can we end with a great sign prominently displayed in front of a Florida funeral home?
- WE WOULD RATHER DO BUSINESS WITH 1,000 AL QAEDA TERRORISTS THAN WITH ONE SINGLE AMERICAN SOLDIER!
  AMEN AND AMEN!!!!!

WORST MUSIC:

Most funerals have music, whether vocal and/or instrumental, live or "canned", music supplied by the funeral home. Sometimes the folks choosing the musical selection are relatives who make great choices but sometimes a family member will "worm" his way into helping the family's decisions. The depth of his musical training might have been a tambourine in the first grade, not to mention having failed the class in common sense. Consider these disasters.

- I heard of a funeral recently where it wasn't enough that the corpse was wheeled into the chapel to the tune of "Send in the Clowns" and then serenaded with "Sweet Georgia Brown", she was wheeled out to "The Party's Over". Worse yet, all of these songs were sung by a 71-year-old warbling woman who reminds you of your Aunt Gladys, accompanying herself on a Hammond organ straight out of your grandmother's 1950s living room.

- Broadway? Dancing? Right on! I heard about a Broadway musical rendition which included a chorus line dancing in front of the open casket to the tune of "Another Opening of Another Show:" After the reading of the obituary, "Somewhere Over the Rainbow" was rendered by a 70+-year-old lady dressed as Judy Garland. (*Bring on the sparkling red Dorothy shoes!*) At the conclusion of the service, people exited the chapel to an up-roaring rendition of "There's No Business Like Show Business". (*Side Note: The organist resigned after this one. Said she couldn't take it anymore. The service the next day was too concluded with "New York, New York.")*

- One woman was called upon to preach the funeral of her own son. After calling him a litany of derogatory names, she proceeded to call her boyfriend (who was younger than her deceased son) to the podium and asked the organist to play a particular song. As the organist played "Amazing Grace" she and her man slow danced in front of her son's casket.

- Many organists may have taken "early retirement" had they been asked to play these selections:

  "Another One Bites the Dust" by Queen
  "Time of Your Life" by Green Day
  "Stayin' Alive" by the Bee Gees
  "Ding Dong, the Witch is Dead" from "The Wizard of Oz"
  "Bury Me Six Feet Under" by Alexandra Burke
  "Bang, Bang, You're Dead" by Dirty Pretty Things
  "Strike up the band!"

PART 4 – EPITAPHS:

DISCLAIMER: Most of these tombstone remarks came from newspapers and unknown sources. Names and locations have been removed.

"The words we want written on our tombstones reflect our deepest values" (From the book, ENCOURAGEMENT, by Rabbi Pliskin).

Death is never a funny thing, but that doesn't mean the tombstones can't be entertaining or even hilarious. Here is a collection of epitaphs that should make you laugh—whether they were meant to be funny or not.

- Here lies an atheist. All dressed up and no place to go.
- Comic: There goes the neighborhood!
- (Comic) I will not be back right after these messages.
- I told you I was sick!
- I came into this world without my permission and I left without it also.
- Here lies one who lived for others; now she has peace and so do they!
- Here lies so-and-so. He was caught with the wife of (name).
- (Name) Here lies an honest lawyer, And that is strange.
- (Name) Two things I love most,
  Good horses and beautiful women,
  And when I die I hope they tan this old hide of mine
  And make it into a lady's riding saddle,
  So I can rest in peace between the two things I love.
- (Name) Born 15 September . . .
  Accidentally shot 4th the following year,
  As a mark of affection from his brother.
- She lived with her husband fifty years
  And died in the confident hope of a better life.
- Here lies (Name). Silent at last.
- HE LOVED BACON

He loved his wife and kids too.
- I was hoping for a pyramid!
- I knew this was going to happen to me!
- I am woman, hear me roar!
  And boy did she!
- Beneath this stone my wife doth lie
  Now she's at rest and so am I.
- Here lies the body of a man who died
  Nobody mourned—nobody cried.
  How he lived, how he fared
  Nobody knows—nobody cared.
- (Name) lies as silent clay
  Who on the 21st of May
  Began to hold her tongue.
- Here's to Johnny, quite a guy
  Very sad he had to die.
  All was well, could not be better
  Till he wrote my girl a letter.

"Honest! I'm Telling the Truth!" (Theme Funerals)

The French author, Jules Renard, said in 1890, "Look for the ridiculous in everything and you will find it!"

No two people grieve the same way, although society can at times try to mandate the norm. Grieving people are likely to allow emotions rather than reason to guide their actions when making funeral arrangements for their loved ones.

One of the current trends in the funeral business is "Theme Funerals." Although rare in some parts of the country, they have sometimes replaced the more traditional funerals that have reigned supreme for years. Mourning is being revolutionized with theme caskets, funeral services, and burial locations. Folks planning their own funerals want to have a service reflecting their life, but also one that will be talked about for years to come. Cookie-cutter funerals are out.

Many today don't want to be locked into tradition, any tradition, even in funeral planning! They want to be different, creative, marching in their own parade. In other words, they enjoy the challenge of trying to swim upstream against society. Thus a "Theme Funeral" appeals to them, at least in planning a family member's service.

Whether it's a traditional funeral, or a "Theme Funeral," there will always be some individuals who will look for the ridiculous in every funeral, and will find it.

I've always told people, "Don't let anyone take away your grief." Remember, no two people, or families grieve the same way, nor do they display it the same way. Normalcy and control that is logical to one may be illogical to another.

The following theme funerals are for real. Information concerning these services has been collected from various sources, including obituaries, funeral directors, newspapers, and personal experiences. All names and locations have been changed, not to protect the deceased, but to protect those who made these arrangements, and those who might be embarrassed by these "productions" and want no part of it. Just keep in mind that we don't all march in the same parade, so enjoy this parade as it passes by.

— Open casket? Not for (*name*). Seems he wanted to be propped up and "standing at his own funeral. When visitors entered the funeral home, they found (*name*) standing up in the visitation room, allowing himself to be photographed with his guests surrounding him.

There was a table nearby with small throw away box cameras if the guests forgot their camera or cell phone. A sign inside a funeral home said, "Help yourself!"

— "Have it your way!" The whole funeral theme was designed after a fast-food chain. On the way to the cemetery, the hearse lead the processional through the drive through window where each guest was served a Whopper hamburger, plus given a second one, "one for the road." as tributes to the deceased. Fries were extra. One large Whopper was placed on the lid of the casket . . . "Have it your way!"

— One lady had no luck while married to the deceased in getting him to darken the doors of the church. When he died she decided to to have a "Spiritual Theme Service" just to spite her late husband. It offered her an opportunity for him not to talk back and complain or make snide remarks. Realizing that he probably would split hell wide open, she believed he had to be baptized to get into heaven. On the way to the cemetery, the funeral procession stopped at her church where the casket was removed and wheeled into the church. You guessed it! Sprinkling wouldn't do. She had her husband's body removed and immersed. Four strong men stepped into the baptism tank carrying the deceased, now removed from his casket, said a few words over him, then lowering him into the water. He went "down dry dead," and came out "dead wet." She was happy!

— In capturing her husband's personality who had been a taxidermist, she transformed the visitation room into a forest with stuffed animals of all kinds in their natural habitats. Birds of all kind were suspended from the ceiling while other animals were perched in trees, some hiding behind bushes. His favorite was the coral Cobra, now posed ready to strike, on the lid of the casket, drawing the most attention. Not only was the snake his favorite piece of work, but it kept the unruly children at a distance.

— One lady belonged to a quilting group of ladies who met every Tuesday. Displayed around the visitation room were samples of Afghans, needle work, quilts, etc. Visitation just happened to be on Tuesday so all the ladies brought their projects with them and had their Tuesday quilting bee seated around the casket, talking and carrying on like nothing was wrong. Light refreshments were also served.

— One man could always be located in his recliner, watching TV, remote control in hand, and drinking beer or eating some snack. So when he died and friends came for visitation, there they found him, seated in his recliner, his feet propped up, a TV in front of him watching a football game, an end table next to his chair loaded with beer bottles and snacks, and the remote control tied to his waist.

– One young man lived to race his Harley Davidson motorcycle wildly and fast until one day a telephone pole and his Harley had an unfortunate meeting. Come visitation, guests found him in full leather gear and helmet, perched astride, leaning forward on a motorcycle.

– One man claimed that he loved Arabian food from a certain restaurant that had live entertainment as well. When he died the visitation room was draped to look like an Arabian tent, with a few Arabian horses out on the front lawn of the funeral home. Not only did he have a native band playing Arabian music but he had belly dancers that performed all evening. The funeral director had a hard time getting people to leave when it came time to close for the evening, especially the men.

– One family, being extremely proud of their father's gold medals and military achievements, not only displayed them proudly, but they turned the visitation room into a war zone. Fox holes, fake blown up buildings and even an old Army Jeep with father sitting behind the wheel were on display. Sound effects of bombs bursting in the distance with red flashes of light were heard ever so often.

– One horse rancher family turned the visitation room into a corral, with bales of hay, a wooden fence with his familiar horse tied to the post. It was originally planned to have him seated on the horse, but several factors nicked that plan. The ceiling was too low for him to be on the horse, but mainly they couldn't keep him from falling off the horse. So they were able to place him on the top rail of the fence next to his tied up horse, and stick a piece of straw in his mouth.

– One gentleman who had been an avid fisherman and hunter had the visitation room looking like a sporting goods store. Instead of a casket, they had a bass boat with him perched on the front seat, fly rod in hand, dressed in his fishing gear, including his special fishing hat, and favorite pipe sticking out of the corner of his mouth.

– The lady was a craft enthusiast. You named it, and she made it. Displayed around the visitation room were samples of all kinds of her craft work and little projects for guests to attempt. What was so unique was that her casket's decorations were almost as colorful as a float in the Macy's Christmas Parade.

– Fortunately for everyone, this particular funeral home was located outside the city limits. When this famous journalist died he had a row of canons lined up outside the funeral home where his ashes were fired out into space to the tune of "Mr. Tambourine Man."

– This city's 4th of July fireworks display was none the wiser. The deceased had arranged in advance, on the side and with a few bucks under the table, to have his ashes placed in one of the largest pieces of fireworks used for the grand finale at this particular firework show. He wanted to go out with a bang was his desire.

– This environmental-conscious individual who just happened to be passionate about skeet shooting arranged to have his ashes placed in a biodegradable helium balloon.

The visitation room took on an environmental theme with gift bags for each visitor consisting of a young tree sapling for planting afterwards, several packages of seeds for future trees, and a coupon for a full bag of all natural fertilizer from Pikes Nursery. After the service, the balloon was launched over the ocean and his buddies shot at the balloon until it burst and scattered his ashes.

— One funeral home has a cookie-scented viewing room affectionately known as "Big Mamma's Kitchen," with a stove, refrigerator, dishes, a can of Crisco, and even faux food.

— One 84 year old man, a diehard Rams fan, asked for a streamer-laden, Super Bowl-style service. Artificial turf marked with yard lines was laid over the carpet. Attendees entered on the 50 yard with the casket set in the end zone. Cheerleaders in their regular cheering outfits lined the hallway on both side leading into the visitation room, while shaking their pom-poms at arriving guests. A free snack bar was located at the end of the hall serving hot dogs and popcorn.

— Another man who loved barbecue arranged for a BBQ Theme with coolers, picnic tables, lawn chairs, and a grill with dry ice so that "smoke" would pour out while the deceased was standing at the grill, completely dressed for grilling. For added effect, a couple of baby pigs, properly contained, were nearby.

A fireman had the visitation room decorated in fire prevention items with a gift bag containing a smoke alarm for each guest. The pall bearers were all dressed in their fire fighting gear. On the way to the cemetery, his casket was placed on top of a fire truck with the sirens blaring.

- An 88 year old prankster, knowing he was dying, asked the help from a friend who waited 2 months after the death, then mailed 34 hand written cards to friends with heaven as the return address.

- One lady had a costume jewelry style party at her visitation. The theme was "Keeping Your Loved Ones Closer." She had each of her closest lady friends pick out a piece of jewelry that would hold a stone in it. Then she had her cremated remains pressed into actual diamonds for the settings. Some had chosen rings, necklaces, and earrings.

- One young man loved kayaking with a passion. His theme was outdoor sports, including a small rock climbing wall, gear, and of course, his favorite kayak with him positioned in it with paddle in hand.

- One elderly gentleman had always wanted to run away with the circus since he was a boy. The visitation room was arranged to look like a big top, including the magical three rings. The minister was dressed as the Ring Master, while the pall bearers were dressed as clowns, full makeup and costumes. Guests were encouraged to dress as circus performers as well, while cotton candy and peanuts were handed out. Instead of traditional church music, a circus calliope was played not only upon the arrival of guests but at various times during the service. Balloons were supplied for everyone! He was then carried to the cemetery on an ornate circus wagon while clowns ran around at the cemetery, squirting people with the flowers they wore on their lapels while one clown made animals out of balloons and gave them to the children.

- The deceased died on the 18th green one Sunday while his family was in church. His children had him cremated and his ashes placed into golf balls. His memorial service was held on the 18th hole, while his buddies lined up and took turns knocking his ashes out into eternity.

— A pilot had been killed in a small plane crash. His eulogy ended as his casket was being placed in the hearse, Frank Sinatra's song being played in the background, "Come Fly With Me..."

— A couple were such fans of Elvis that they had one complete room in their home with nothing but items related to the late singer. It was a shrine! When the husband died, his theme funeral was to pay homage to Elvis, with everything "Elvis" down to his music, and including several performing Elvis impersonators.

— You like Christmas? So did this particular family. The casket arrived at the church atop a full size "Santa sled" being pulled by pall bearers dressed in reindeer outfits. The church was decorated in full Christmas mode, including dozens of various Christmas trees, gaily wrapped presents, and scores of individuals dancing down the aisle in gingerbread man costumes, elves, etc. It was like Disney on Parade.

— A well known neighborhood boxer died, and for his theme, a boxing ring was built in the visitation room. He was placed standing in the corner of the ring, dressed in his bright yellow boxing robe and hood, boxing gloves and shoes, wearing his traditional sunglasses. Fans/guests were invited to have their picture taken with him.

— Not wanting a typical grieving funeral for their son, who was a well known basketball player, they had him dressed in his uniform, seated in a chair, watching one of his games on a TV. The rest of the room was decorated as a sports bar, with various TVs playing various games their son had played in. Chicken wings and cold beer were served as well.

— A young man was a well-liked violinist who played with a group of chamber musicians. He was placed in a chair with his violin under his chin, surround by other members of the chamber group, while they played music as guests arrived.

Did you find the ridiculous here? Or the sublime?

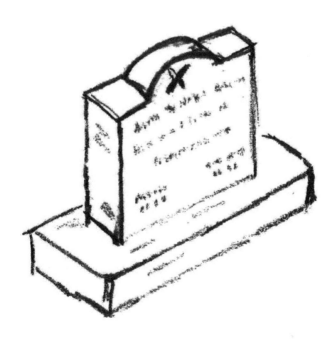

"What a Trip!"

"How to meet your next mate at the last one's funeral," is clearly a "NO! NO!" if you're concerned with proper funeral home etiquette. "There is such a thing?" you might ask. Trust me, there is and a funeral is not potentially a dating service.

For centuries people have always used funerals to search for prospects even before internet dating services were all the rage. It has almost been a tribal thing even before the last mate is in the ground. Some have even gone so far as labeling it as "scouting out the competition" . . . interpretation . . . "What are my odds? Do I or do I not?" How do I know this is true? I've officiated at scores of funerals in my lifetime and I've observed human nature in hot pursuit.

Some people's actions would put you to shame.

Not only have I observed human nature at work as an adult, but as a 10 year old boy I lived out a classic example of desperate people in desperate times, doing desperate things. Any psychology magazine would have been proud of me had it been available. All we need in my recounting this story is a little bit of "Mission Impossible" music in the background for setting the mood. It was one of the worst of times, the hottest of times in August . . . and so the story goes!

With a well-developed imagination for a 10 year old boy, I

recall riding in the back window ledge of my dad's 1940 Ford, (*before seat belts were ever thought* of) on the hottest day in August, heading below the Mason Dixie Line because Grandmother #2 had passed. What she had passed wasn't quite clear to me. One minute I heard my parents say she had died, the next, I heard she had passed. As far as I was concerned, being an authority on the game of Monopoly, she could have passed "Go" and collected $200 dollars.

My next question almost caused my dad to drive the car off the road, when suddenly I innocently brought up what we had done with my pet goldfish when it had died. You would have thought I had committed a "Cardinal Sin", when all I was doing was offering some advice on what they could do with Grandma since they couldn't get their story straight. Did she die or pass?

For once, one of my many questions didn't spark the same response I normally received from my father, "Go ask your mother!" All I remember was hearing my mother say under her breath, "It's your turn!" Regardless of what grandma might have passed, I just knew we were headed below the Mason Dixie Line which meant to me we were crossing the border into some foreign country. Thankfully I didn't have to get any shots like some foreign missionaries I had heard about.

Based on my Sunday school training, this Mason Dixie Line thing had to be close to the gates of hell. The further south we got, the hotter it became, and I knew it wouldn't be long before we'd be smelling smoke. Mother Nature was our only source of air conditioning as it (*along with seat belts*) hadn't been invented.

Riding with all the windows down had its benefits, regardless of the pending smell of smoke. One benefit of no air conditioning was that we only heard half of what our parents were instructing my little brother and me. Regardless, with "Are we almost there?" every few miles, we seemed to get the same lecture of what to do, and what not to do, with threats of our early demise if we did or didn't. You would have thought we were escapees, or the world's most dangerous convicts!

Later that night, with my brother asleep in the back seat of the car, I left my coveted position in the back window of our old Ford, and stood behind my parents' seat for a clearer view of what the headlamps might discover for my inquisitive mind. I just knew we would be crossing the Mason Dixie Border any moment with its border patrol guards, guns and all, and we would have to get out of the car, spread eagle our legs, and be patted down. I couldn't wait!

It was going to be so neat! But alas, all that transpired was Mom talking about an Ina Faye and something about her having the "call," and she wondered had she called this person and that person, and would there be enough food, and, etc. etc., you know, boring stuff to me. All I wanted was to see the border crossing police. I had already planned what I was going to share when school started in September, when "What did you do this summer?" was our first assignment.

With the vision of being stopped by the border patrol fading fast, all I could think of now was how many people were going to be at Paw Paw's to see what Grandmother had passed. I just hoped it wasn't painful, whatever it was, or had she just died? I was also concerned that someone wouldn't mess up and do to Grandmother #2 what I had done to Reggie my goldfish when he died. After my dad's lecture number 637 I knew that wasn't a good idea. He reassured me that wouldn't happen since the facilities out back were not flushable.

With my little brother asking for the one hundred millionth time, "Are we almost there?" I quickly reminded him of what lay ahead. "So don't rush it!" We would soon be experiencing pats on the top of our heads and backsides, pinches on the cheeks, followed by, "My, haven't you grown," from people we didn't know but were told we did.

"Can't we just settle for a pat down by real police at the border, and just skip this family pat-down thing?" he asked. Being the older and wiser brother, I had to sadly break the news to him that it appeared this wasn't going to be possible, so buck up, be a man, and face the unalterable!

The "call" was an important function of any well-planned community funeral, wedding, or reunion. Forget Bar Mitzvahs right now. It was the 40s and this was the Bible Belt. The Baptists and Methodists normally couldn't get along with each other unless there was the "call". The word itself was almost a magical one that drew both sides together in sharing a common denominator. For the current electronic generation to fully understand what the "call" was, a time-warp example is needed.

I must remind the reader that this was a very small town. In fact, to even call it that would be greatly understating the obvious. There was no town square, not even a statue of any kind, making it a pigeon-free zone. In fact, if you were seated on the wrong side of the Greyhound Bus when it passed through the town, you would have missed it. This "bustling municipality" consisted of Gus's Filling Station out on the hard road, the one-room post office held up on cement blocks and Hazel's General Store where sliced baloney was 5 cents a pound. A dime's worth could feed a family of 6 for a week with enough of the pull-away rind to feed the dogs as well. Communication among the residents? No email? No FAX? No cell phone?

Unlike today's private cell phone world, in those days it wasn't uncommon for as many as fourteen or more individuals to be on the same phone line, called a party line. Each party had its own bell ring, which meant all parties could identify who was receiving an incoming call and could listen in on the conversations if desired. All did listen in but would deny it to their dying days. The funny part was that people, on hearing the bell ring of their neighbors, would wait a few seconds and then slowly pick up the receiver, thinking no one would know they were listening in. The truth was that when their receiver was lifted, a clicking sound was heard all down the line!

In this small community, there was a self-appointed "Queen of the Calls" by the name of Sister Ina Faye, a more proper name being "Information Central," "Command Center" or "Mother Superior of Gossip". In this small hamlet, there was no television or daily newspaper available for information, only the radio, or Mother Superior of Gossip. Many had experienced her wrath, having denied her the respect and homage she felt she was due. It wasn't beneath her to turn her umbrella into a deadly weapon and give a gentle poke in the ribs to get the attention of the guilty. She had even gone so far as to deliver a slap or two. Of course, they were love pats, according to her.

This "call" from "Command Center" was the forerunner of our modern day "Amber Alert."

It was alerting all the potential matrimonial prospects, that my grandfather's second wife had died, or passed "Go" or something. Could this possibly be an open door for #3 if their cards were played right? It was an alert call that this could be the "last chance" for some, and it could escalate into a royal battle to the altar. Be prepared!

To those who were still married, it announced that it was another battle cry over who would bring the best-fried chicken or green bean casserole with mushroom soup, (if the general store could get it), covered in corn flakes, or crumbled cornbread to the wake. Not only did this "call" affect young and old, single and married, but included the chickens in the front yard, who by now were trying to hide. To the single, it was the special ingredient in their casserole that might help take them down the aisle at a later date. All was fair in love and fried chicken.

Regardless, before my Paw Paw would "cross over," die, or pass, there was a flip side to this story, a flaw which would follow him all the days of his life. He couldn't stay married. His grand total of four wives all died on him, and he was headed for #5 until he was halted in his tracks by "Mr. Health Issues," and three determined daughters who proclaimed loud and clear, "enough is enough!'

It was well rumored that if a lady desired to be his next wife, she had to have a "death wish," and she best have her affairs in order for she was soon to check out.

What was even more confusing to my tender age was that it was said that every one of them died of natural causes. Pray tell! How can this thing called death, passed, or whatever you wanted to call it, be natural? There's nothing natural about death. You don't see them walking around, talking, eating and doing what a grandma is supposed to do, regardless of what number she might be!

As a 10-year-old boy, I was experiencing the happenings around the passing of #2 and would be watching those vying for #3 position. From all outward appearance and gossip, it promised to be the dress rehearsal for the Battle of Armageddon. Reason? Leading the pack of "hopefuls" was none other than Sister Ina Faye, the terror of the town who, up to this point, had been unsuccessful in getting any man to the altar.

How do I know all of this? Forget that I'm just 10? I had learned early in life that if I really wanted to know what was going on, what Mom and Dad were thinking, or hiding from me, I just had to pretend I was asleep. Works every time! So putting that technique into play, I pretended to be asleep in the back seat of the car on our long trip in crossing the Mason Dixie Border. This technique works quite well most of the time, but I had to listen very closely this time because of the car windows being down. The cool night air felt good, but it played havoc on my trying to get all the details. But I heard enough to know that I wanted nothing to do with this woman, and I would fill in the gaps, I said to myself when we come face to face.

But what I did hear, loud and clear that made my toenails curl and send shivers up my spine and not from the cold night air, was my dad saying, "Even the devil forks his tail and heads for the hills at just the mention of her name." If Sister Ina Faye was way too much even for the devil to handle, what was I getting myself into? Better yet, who was this "She Devil" that was trying to land position #3?

Before drifting off to sleep with the sweet hum of the night air, I had convinced myself that I had heard enough to know this Sister Woman wasn't even coming close to my Paw Paw if I could help it! Political correctness hadn't yet been invented, but it was my honor and duty to protect my Paw Paw from the hooks of this wicked woman.

Making sure my pad and pencil were nearby, (my tools for collecting secret spy information on this "Sister Woman") I drifted off to a much-needed rest. Hours later, which seemed like only a few minutes, I was awakened by, "Wake up, Son. We're here." Being greeted by hot sticky sunshine streaming in through the open window, I quickly asked myself, "Where is the air?" We had arrived in what was referred to as the Promised Land? All I could think was if this is the Promised Land, someone forgot to turn the heat down!

Climbing out of the backseat of the car and looking around, I would later in life describe it as a Norman Rockwell painting. To my young mind, it was just a bunch of people trying to stay cool in the August 90 degree-plus weather. There were cars parked everywhere, people standing on the front porch fanning themselves while holding a glass of iced tea. A handkerchief was the tool of necessity for almost everyone, some constantly wiping their brows, others using them as substitute fans. Under every tree in the front yard was a circle of folding chairs from the funeral home, where people sat talking quietly while trying to stay cool in the shade.

After all the patting on the top of our heads, knowing we were at least several inches shorter after enduring "My, my, haven't you grown?" numerous times, we obviously were getting a bad case of cooties! There was no way of getting around it.

By this time my brother had made a third-removed-distant-cousin-friend (*I wasn't even going to try and figure out that "third removed" thing when he was standing right before us!*) and was headed for the hayloft. Myself, breaking free from relatives I didn't know or care to know, I was free to circle and listen in on conversations, all the while writing things in my little pad I'm sure my parents didn't want me to know . . . Mission Impossible had begun.

Suddenly, flying up the long drive that led to the farmhouse, nearly breaking the sound barrier, was what appeared to be the Titanic on wheels. As it roared into the front yard, it was plain to see it was a big old Buick Roadmaster car making my father's Ford look the size of a circus clown's car. Behind it trailed a whirlwind of dust capable of wiping out not only Kansas but Paw Paw's farm as well.

Screeching to a sudden stop, without taking out a fleeing chicken, was "Information Central," Mother Superior of Gossip. I would soon learn this was the enemy I was taking down. The atmosphere suddenly became dead silent, being replaced with the sound of air being sucked out of everyone's lungs in spite of the 98-degree weather. No one moved, birds stopped chirping, hens stopped laying, and playing children suddenly became statues. Even the cows in the nearby field all looked toward the farmhouse and hung their heads in unison. I later heard that some of the cows' milk had turned to cottage cheese at milking time due to fright!

When the dust had settled and I could see clearly, standing beside her car, posing in a position that said, "I'm here," stood the "She Devil." It was the least offensive name I had heard that afternoon and I had written it down. I knew I had to tear that page out of my little pad. If my parents had ever found it, there wouldn't have been a "go ask your mother (*or father*); it would be a race between the two of them for a bar of soap and my little mouth would never be the same! But in the wake of Sister Ina Faye's grand entrance, you could see the facial expressions of the other candidates for wife #3 melting away, yet not quite ready to admit defeat. Although I had a spark of sympathy for the losers, my mission was to protect my Paw Paw, whom I loved dearly. My eyes squinting, setting my jaw, I said to myself like any good 10-year-old spy on a life or death mission, "Bring it on, sister! You're going down!"

I slowly cased my soon-to-be-victim, from top to bottom, a method I had learned from the back of a Captain Winnie cereal box. She was dressed in total black, from top to bottom including black gloves. Can you believe gloves in 90-degree weather? I asked myself. This convinced me that she was determined not to leave any fingerprints at the scene of the crime.

These people below the Mason Dixie Border sure dress funny! Her large wide-brimmed hat was covered in a black veil that made her look like a bee farmer, causing me to wonder what she was hiding under that dark veil. Maybe it was a blessing and not a curse that we didn't know what she looked like in real life! Maybe she should be encouraged to keep that veil pulled down, but time would tell! One could only say "She Devil" was dressed for a mission . . . to get herself a man!

The crowd parted, giving Sister Ina Faye a wide berth as she waved her regal wave and nodded to selected individuals on her way to her goal: Paw-Paw who was standing on the front porch. Her actions said, "He's all mine! Sorry girls, but I've got this one! I'm soon to be wife #3." Some were cheering her on, hoping she would become wife #3, taking her out of circulation permanently. There were some benefits to this "death wish" thing!

It was obvious that her earlier attempts to snag a man and getting one down to the altar had failed. But this time she had pulled out all the stops to meet Paw-Paw, as she carried her famous, in her own mind, green bean casserole with mushroom soup and smothered in corn flakes, like this was the "crown jewel". She extended her outward dramatic sympathies for all her subjects to hear, while jumping for joy on the inside as her head spun with future wedding plans.

Later that evening as the mosquitoes accepted their responsibility of driving everyone back into the house, but avoiding the men on the front porch (*who produced their own smoke screen of protection*), I found the ladies who were not members of Ina Faye's fan club. They were secretly giving pep talks to the other candidates not to give up their pursuit.

I wandered freely, unattended, which should never be allowed to happen to a 10 year old boy, especially one with pad in hand, on a mission, and with an imagination as big as all outdoors. This could prove to be dangerous!

Pausing at the large food table, I surveyed the items, noticing especially the mounds of fried chicken which must have depleted the chicken population in the area. My main goal was looking for a green bean casserole with corn flakes which would stand out because most were covered with crumbed corn bread. (*It was during the war and only those who knew somebody who knew somebody were able to get corn flakes.*) I was totally convinced that hers was poisonous because the "She Devil" had made it! (*Actually, I wouldn't touch that stuff no matter what, and anyone crazy enough to eat it, poisoned or not, deserved to experience their final moments then and there!*) I knew for sure she didn't care who she poisoned, just as long as she got her man. Looking back, I realize my young spy-investigation-crazy logic was no good! There was no poison in her casserole! If Paw-Paw ate some of her "poisoned" casserole, she would destroy her own plan for being #3. Disregarding any logic, and to be on the safe side, my plan was still on line to knock that casserole onto the floor, thus saving a complete community from a sure death.

Before I could execute my plan and finish my inspection of the food table, from out of nowhere came this dark, deep voice from behind me, sending me into complete shock and years of therapy. It was none other than the veiled "She Devil." With one swoop of her long boney arm and fingers, she picked up a plate, filled it with her green bean casserole, and shoved it into my hand and said, with final authoritarian tone, "Eat this, kid! Don't waste it! It's your Paw- Paw's favorite!"

Was she trying to impress me? If she was, it wasn't working. I've got your number, I thought to myself. "You're trying to poison me," I shouted as I shot out the door looking for the safety of my father's arms.

Paw-Paw's house was a large two story brick farm house, a haunted-looking structure at best, with a large attic where I knew lived the ghosts and goblins of the past. My imagination told me it was possible that Captain Hook's ghost lived up there. During the day I never ventured beyond the second floor, because I knew I never would return. And now that it was evening, they had turned down the lights even lower and were now calling it a "wake", where people talked in soft whispers and I just knew in every dark shadow lurked a ghost of the past.

In those days a visitation at a funeral home was unheard of. The deceased was always brought home for this thing they called a "wake". To make room for the casket, the furniture was either rearranged or moved out on the front porch. The undertaker even brought two pink pole lights (*if electricity was available*) to make grandma look "rite purdy". If it was extremely hot, as it was that summer, he would bring several fans to turn on the deceased.

As a young child, I couldn't figure that one out. Grandma wasn't sweating but everyone else was. The other mystery that confused me was this thing they called a wake where everyone had to sit up with Grandma. Where did they think she was going? The word "wake" was now lined up next to those other confusing words, "passing," "passed," "died," "asleep in Jesus," or "She's gone to be with Jesus."

That one had confused me beyond comprehension. And if she had died and gone to heaven, why was she still lying there in the parlor? Were people whispering because Grandma was asleep and they didn't want to wake her up? When I checked this afternoon she was still asleep. Why were they sitting up all night with her? She wasn't going anywhere, or were they keeping her from going to see Jesus? This "asleep in Jesus," caused me to search for Jesus, (*except in the attic!*) with no luck. Where was He? The only evidence that He had been there was that He left a lot of funeral home fans with His picture on them, which was a constant reminder that I had better behave myself. But I would like to know where they got those big popsicles because those sticks glued to the back of the fans were monsters!

As the wake continued I saw a most interesting sight. Seated in a single row of chairs in the parlor, fanning themselves with their best crocheted handkerchiefs, were all the "hopeful wanna-be's" of the hamlet, each hoping to be the next Mrs. Paw Paw. (*Forget the life expectancy thing!)* They were all dressed to the nines in their funeral black dresses, some even wearing black hats and black gloves to match their black shoes. If a storm took out the electricity, you could possibly lose a whole row of ladies in the dark!

The room smelled of sashay powder, mixed with the fragrance of mothballs, with enough gardenia powder to keep them from "perspiring." (*Horses sweat, southern ladies perspire!*) I just knew if the funeral home fans got turned the wrong directions and the air hit these ladies by surprise, there would be a gardenia storm of sashay powder that could compete with any sandstorm in Arizona, as well as wipe out the mosquito population for weeks.

While "circling the wagons" of possible matrimony, each lady would delicately gossip about anything and everything that might elevate her in the mind of Paw Paw. Meanwhile, I secretly wrote in my little pad, potential ammunition to sabotage anyone from being wife #3, especially the She Devil. They would sit with Grandma for awhile, then get up and flit around the room, always making sure their path took them within the vicinity of Paw-Paw. "Can I get you something to eat? You must keep up your strength! Coffee?" Then they would end up back in the parlor with Grandma, Guardians of Grief in case they were needed to comfort someone.

As the evening progressed, the gossip got juicier and juicier and more and more clothing was removed, until by morning the black hats and gloves were off, and shame of all shame, we even saw a bit of ankle. You knew their corsets were killing them! No matter how large the pot of gold was at the end of this rainbow, they secretly longed for the morning to arrive.

AUTHOR'S POST SCRIPT: Paw-Paw didn't start dating and looking for wife #3 until two and a half years later, having sold his farm and moving to a nearby county. Wife #3 lived longer than #2 but not as long as #1, my "original Grandma".

Sister Ina Faye, alias "She Devil, Mother Superior of Gossip" continued to have no luck making it to the altar.

She finally entered a convent and became a nun, rising to the position of a "living lesson" for the other nuns on how to practice patience without destroying their religious vows in the process. Rumor has it that over half of the nuns have left the convent for various reasons but all giving credit for their new lives to Sister Ina Faye.

*This chapter is in no way a reflection on the single women of our day. Many have chosen to remain single and have made significant contributions to society.

"It Gets Better!"

Before the sun came up, the farm animals had been milked and fed and the house was now abuzz with activity in preparation for the funeral service, but not before a hearty breakfast was served. The room smelled of fresh brewing coffee, eggs and bacon on the wood-burning stove, popping and cracking and causing us to wonder, "How much longer?"

After getting our fill of a great breakfast, my brother and I weren't prepared for the next event in our young lives. We were told to go to the back porch and strip down. Strip down? Here? Now? There in the middle of the porch was a large wash tub filled with iceberg water. "Get in," came the order from Mother.

This whole thing had to be some ancient tribal ritual below the Mason-Dixie Border. "And don't you dare get dirty before we go to the church!" It wasn't a suggestion, but a command and the tone of Mother's voice spoke volumes. "If you do I'll tan your hide so hard you won't be able to sit down for a week."

For reinforcements, she called in the big guns, DAD! "Do something useful besides drink coffee and swap fishing stories with the men," she barked at Dad. "Make sure the boys don't get dirty!"

As we left for the funeral home, my mind began its usual whirl. Has anyone ever noticed that undertakers hardly ever smile, and their facial expressions are always as if they're the ones who have just lost the loved one? When they do speak, the tone of their voices is so low I just know the katydids stop rubbing their legs together, trying to hear what's being said. Just something else I must ask Paw Paw about, I thought to myself.

Another mind-blowing question began to surface. Once they had all the cars lined up in what they called a "Funeral Procession", they stuck a flag on the front fender of each car that proudly said, "Funeral!" Now tell me . . . as if anybody seeing a hearse pass by with a casket in the back, would think it was anything else?

I know I was experiencing my first funeral and especially one below the Mason Dixon line, but really? This one thing in my advanced 10-year-old mind was the stupidest thing and I'm making a note for sure to ask Paw-Paw. They had everyone in broad daylight turn on their car lights. Have you ever heard of anything as dumb as that? Did the funeral director think we couldn't find our way to the church even in full bright sunshine?

What I did think was pretty neat was as we traveled to the church, oncoming traffic would pull over to the side of the road. My father said it was in respect to the deceased. I had once seen something like that on a News Reel at the movies. Some Queen was passing by and waving at people so I asked Mom if we should wave at those pulling over. I quickly learned that wasn't such a good idea. It had to be the heat that made her so cranky.

The church bell was sounding its mournful toll as the funeral procession pulled up in front of the little old one-room church house, resting gingerly upon what appeared to be large rocks. At least it provided cool shade for a couple of hound dogs, and some loosely wandering chickens who had survived this funeral reprise.

"NO!" was followed by the enforcing hand to my shoulder, "You can't ring the bell, or pet the dogs!" When that hand suddenly appeared out of nowhere landing on my shoulder, I knew if I wanted to see the sunset that evening, I better obey, ask no questions, and begging would only get me closer to my . . . "Yes, Dad," I replied, wondering how he knew what I was about to ask.

We followed Grandma's casket down the center aisle, while everyone in the church stood. I started to ask if we should wave since we didn't wave at those in the cars coming over here when I felt that reassuring hand on my shoulder. "That wouldn't be such a good idea!"

We remained standing while they opened Grandma's casket. I just knew she was relieved to get some fresh air, regardless of how hot it was. There's not much room to move around in those caskets, let alone any ventilation if you know what I mean.

But I was wrong! I later learned the reason that Grandma's casket was left open was that Southerners get suspicious if they close it. They suspect foul play. Also, a closed casket in a small town launches a scandal for sure!

As "The Sweet Bye and Bye" began, I realized it was coming from a desperately out of tune piano being attacked by a little old lady who was hunkered down over the keyboard, daring anyone to come near her territory. It was the cue for those wanting to sing to come up out of the audience and meet in the choir loft. The only words I heard coming from them were, "We shall meet on that beautiful shore." Whenever or wherever we were going, the word "shore" assured me there would be water, and I needed some. What really confused me was, "Some golden daybreak, Jesus will come..." I knew it, my mind whirled. He's ticked off that all these people have those funeral fans with His picture on them and He's coming after them, large popsicle sticks and all!

I cannot think of anything more miserable for a 10-year-old boy than being made to sit up straight in one of those old hard-back church pews, sweat running down his back as the temperature kissed 100 degrees, waiting for the "Sweet By and By" to happen. It had to be the precursor to water boarding that I was experiencing. Being forced to sit between a set of parents, who had pre-warned my brother and me, "Don't you dare make a move! Do you hear me?"

I knew I saw flames shooting out of their nostrils to emphasize their point, and when I experienced that, I best pay attention.

"I mean it," she continued, with a finger pointed in my face for emphasis. Mother always loved to use object lessons with her demands, "Don't you even breathe! If you do, you'll wish you hadn't!" How could I, with their fingers placed on either one of my thighs, ready to launch a pinch if I dare moved or reacted to what was going on in this funeral service. Or should I say, "ritual." It was called a funeral, south of the border, "Mason-Dixon Line Funeral." Regardless, it made me know that, come September, no "What did you do this summer?" would ever be believed. I knew I was doomed from the start.

My brother and I weren't the only ones who had been placed on a strict code of conduct. Paw Paw had made sure that his three daughters, including my mom who always started things, were seated by their husbands and not each other. They were not allowed to sit next to each other for fear the "dreaded giggle loop" would begin. One sister would softly giggle about something until it would be passed on, building in intensity from sister to sister. This would start the giggle looping and looping until it developed into full disastrous laughter.

There I sat, wide-eyed, under the death penalty threat if I breathed. But I soon observed the "entertainment" of the day. There up in front, for all to see was a bald-headed, five-by-five preacher yelling, spitting, sobbing, more than my dog ever thought of doing, and stomping at what must be a bug-infested church.

For emphasis, he waved his Bible in the air. I was not able to completely figure that one out, as most people use fans, but not him. He used his Bible, fanning his way back and forth across the front of the church. I just knew at any moment there was the possibility of Grandma sitting up in her casket and telling that preacher to hold it down because she was trying to sleep.

He was a fire and brimstone preacher, whose job it appeared was to scare the wits out of the mourners and make them feel they were next. Not only did I have that on my mind, but I remembered the church was balancing on large corner rocks. With his stomping back and forth I just knew we were about to experience the "Baptist

Earthquake" of the century, finding ourselves down at the foot of the hill. If you think I was sweating, you should have seen that preacher's face. It was so red I knew at any moment he was going to explode, and I wasn't gonna help clean up the mess. If he was that stupid to carry on like that in a 100-degree temperature, then be my guest. I would think he would at least stop and wring out that handkerchief he profusely tortured. He was sweating so much he looked like someone had thrown him in the river. Was he the result of that song we had just sung, "Shall We Gather at the River"? The reality that I must have nodded off and we had gone down to the river, and I had missed it wasn't a pleasant thought. My only hope of cooling off, gone! Now I'm really gonna be mad at myself because I was so hot.

The preacher began his message by pointing to Grandma in the casket by say, "That dere, is not a purdy site, but she's now got a Gah-LOOOH-rious new body in heaven."

"Now wait a minute," I almost shouted, but quickly was made aware of fingers pressing against my thighs, acting as the first warning shot to be fired. "Don't even think about it!"

I wanted to ask the preacher if she's got a new body, how am I gonna recognize her when I do find her in heaven? He then went on to confuse my educated mind with, "She's absent from the body, present with the Lord." With that, I started to rise a bit off the pew only to be reminded of what was on either side of me. How can Grandma be with the Lord, while she's lying a few feet from me?

People below the Mason-Dixon Line sure get worked up over this funeral stuff, I thought. I just knew I had a lot of questions to ask my Paw-Paw and I knew he would have the answers.

With the heat taking over my attention span, my imagination took over. It was a place where I could escape to and not be bothered by all of the double talk adults come up with. I could ask my own questions, and if I felt like it, answer them as well or make something up.

So I shifted my thoughts to the starting of school, only a few short weeks away. Come this September when the teacher has us write or tell "How I Spent My Summer," she will never believe me, let alone my classmates. Miss Snodgrass (*my new 5th-grade teacher. "Lord, forgive me for the nasty thoughts I have of her before I even step foot in her classroom!"*) will swear I'm lying! I can hear her yelling, "You're making that stuff up!" And the few friends I do have left after hearing about my summer will contemplate whether or not to remain friends with a lunatic. How can I convince her that you can't make this stuff up?

How do I know she'll react like that? Anybody who wears a black dress smelling like mothballs all year long, with black orthopedic shoes and her hair tied up in a knot perched on the back of her head like some lightning rod, might be your first clue as to her way of thinking.

She was known for carrying a ruler in her hand (*straight out of the Gestapo*) and was not afraid to use it! Not getting out much, she lives vicariously through our summer experiences. Without question, everyone knew Miss Snodgrass was capable of ensuring bodily harm with that instrument of doom, known to most of us as a ruler. Her students always said that when she stood next to your desk, peering down over the top of her dirty glasses resting on the end of her nose, slowly slapping that ruler in the palm of her hand . . . you best be caught up, confessed up, and any other "up's" because you were about to meet your maker. I knew that if she didn't finish the job of getting me there, my father would finish the job when I got home from school!

I could strategize about using my sleigh-like desk lid to hide behind, but one look inside told me there was no way in God's blue heaven I could get my now "pubertizing" (*Don't know if there is such a word, but I made it up!*) growing body inside that little space as an attempt of escape.

I dreaded that September's assignment because I always felt the teacher was just being downright nosy as to what we did while out of her sight for three months. I just knew in my case, Miss Snodgrass was sniffing out information to build a case against me the first time I got into trouble in school. My reputation must have preceded me! So, based on that premise, I'm convinced she's up to no good with that upcoming assignment!

My world of imagination was suddenly shattered, either by the noise coming from the back of the church, or what happened with my family. Suddenly the pew shifted, almost turning over, as my parents, Paw Paw and his other two daughters and their husbands, all in unison, whirled around, almost knocking me off the pew into the middle of the floor.

Six little elderly ladies were attempting to make their way up the center aisle, in fact, the only aisle in the church to speak of. They were dressed alike, except for the aprons they wore, some colorfully adorned in various badges and ribbons, wearing their sailor hats, some loaded with pins.

Leading the pack, carrying a pathetic specimen of a homemade funeral wreath, was the spokesman of the group. Looking at each of the little ladies, I just knew that any day above the dirt was a good day for them.

I knew this wasn't part of the service, as I saw Preacher Man, who had already sat down behind the pulpit, suddenly peering around it like a child playing peek-a-boo, obviously in total confusion. I could read his mind from the expression on his face, "How dare you step on my just-finished-great performance."

Before Paw-Paw and his three daughters could even close their mouths from the shock of what had just happened, the entourage of ladies, now assembled across the front of the platform, began their presentation. Although the leader's voice was soft and hard to hear at times, one word came across loud and clear, "Star," causing a massive explosion of emotions from the back of the church.

Again, with the pew almost tipping over with whiplash speed with everyone turning around, we saw Sister, as she liked to be called, waving her handkerchief as if trying to cast out something or get someone's attention. The room vibrated with her shouts of something about a holy ghost, which threw me for a loop. If this room had ghosts in it, as did the attic at Paw-Paw's house, I was out of there. Feeling a strong hand on my shoulder let me know that I didn't need a large PA system announcing to me, "You're going nowhere!"

The entourage of elderly ladies, not a bit phased by the commotion from the back, continued with their presentation, announcing that they were there just as friends of Grandmother, to help her cross the desert of time. Something else confused me about that "Star" again. I wanted to stand and say, if they were following some star, looking for Jesus, they were a bit too late. The Wise Men had already found Him.

The service suddenly ended with the announcement about a "Jericho March." I guess Preacher Man had had enough interruptions for one day. But a Jericho March? In this weather? Now I was really confused and upset, we couldn't "Gather at the River," to cool off, just sing about it, but in 100-degree weather we were going to have a march? As I recalled from my Sunday school lessons, they marched around the city seven times for seven days. And he's sweating now? What is he gonna be like after the march?

Mother, seeing the confusion on my face, leaned over and whispered in my ear that it wasn't a literal march, not to worry. The ladies of the church would one by one come up front, select a floral arrangement, announce to the congregation who it was from, then carry all of them outside, lining the sidewalk on both sides for the casket to pass between on its way to the awaiting hearse.

Once they had placed Grandmother in the hearse, the flowers were literally rammed into the back of the hearse by those soft-spoken-no-expression undertakers, crushing and mutilating them. I could hear Mother gasping and grinding her teeth, a sound I had learned years ago announced that she was about to explode and I best pay attention. When our baseball landed in one of her flower beds back home, it almost took an act of Congress to get it out; she was that protective of her flowers.

Before getting into our car, I looked for the hound dogs, wondering if I dare pet them. But the strongest temptation was the rope hanging in the doorway that rang that big church bell.

Would it be worth just one pull for not seeing the sunset

tonight? Then I heard as well as felt the "death grip" on my shoulder, "Don't you dare! Get in the car!"

Arriving at the grave site, the service was short and to the point. The preacher, his energy now spent, or maybe thinking of that fried chicken that awaited everyone back at the house, hurried through the service. All I remember him saying, as I was looking around at the various tombstones, was "Ashes to ashes and dust to dust..." Feeling a gentle hand on the back of my head, we bowed our heads and prayed.

There were the normal hugs and kisses that are exchanged after a committal service, as people quickly gathered into their cars and left, trying to escape the heat. They all falsely vowed to get together on some other occasion than a funeral and to stay in touch.

There we stood, the immediate family, alone. Looking around I saw the funeral home people along with the gravediggers standing at a distance, giving us all the time we needed. Standing next to the resting casket on the bier stood my Paw-Paw. I suddenly noticed something that I hadn't ever seen my Paw-Paw do. Leaning forward, he placed a rose on the casket, and then he stood up tall as tears welled up in his eyes and slowly trickled down his cheeks. My Paw-Paw was crying and I felt helpless!

After waiting a few minutes, I walked over and, standing next to him, placed my small arm around his waist, and laid my head against his arm. It was one of those moments when words are absent and would be meaningless if available.

It was only that silent presence that would bring a moment of comfort with those inaudible words, "I'm here with you, Paw-Paw!" Slowly he turned around and softly said, "Let's go!" And then it was over. That's it? I thought to myself. What happens next?

"The Real Me"

The breezes coming through the car windows as we drove back to the farm may have brought a moment of relief from the 100-degree weather, but it did very little, if anything, to soothe our grieving hearts. Things had changed. Things were not the same. The parlor furniture that had been stored on the front porch was now back where it belonged. The vast number of folding chairs that had been on loan from the funeral home was gone as well.

A few friends and family members greeted us as we arrived. There were hugs and soft words spoken, followed by pats on the back, as they gently led us into the house where the "post-funeral" reprise awaited us. It's a well-known fact that nobody eats better than a bereaved Southerner, and friends had not failed us this time either. Every good Southern woman is known for and required to have a funeral food specialty that would be placed among the (*practically mandatory*) green bean casseroles, deviled eggs, cold fried chicken, and plenty of sweet tea.

How did I know this? I had learned very early in life that there were special casserole dishes that were just for "funeral food," because my mother's name had been printed on the bottom of the dish. That marked that dish as something almost "holy," special, separate from the norm and that should not be messed with if you expected to see the sunrise the next morning. There were several reasons for their names to be printed on the bottom of the casserole dish, but the main one was that the family would know to whom the dish should be returned.

While enjoying the reprise of special foods that friends and loved ones had prepared, you could hear stories about the deceased being shared, with the occasional laughter breaking the moment of grieving. Someone would remember an incident concerning the loved one who had passed and smiles would cross the faces as they added their stories as well. Regardless, it just didn't seem the same. Grandma was not there!

Later that afternoon, Paw-Paw didn't have to ask me twice to walk with him down by the pond where, without notice he picked me up and flung me high into the air, landing me in the middle of the pond. Resurfacing from the cold depths of the pond, I was greeted by what I thought was the world's largest cannon ball, called Paw-Paw. I just knew he had emptied out half of the pond.

After spending some quality time alone with this best friend, Paw-Paw and I were summoned and told that it was time to get out of the water; we were going back to the cemetery one more time. When I asked why, I was gently reminded by my mother that we were going back home tomorrow, up north, and . . . she choked up and was unable to finish.

Upon arriving back at the grave site I wasn't prepared for what awaited me. There was no casket, just a mound of dirt with a few flowers piled every which way on top of the dirt. Where was Grandma? What had they done with her?

After the family members had rearranged the flowers and made small talk, little by little they walked away among the other tombstones, observing and making comments about each one, leaving Paw-Paw and me the only ones standing by Grandma's grave.

Tears began to well up in my eyes as I stared at the mound of dirt. Where's Grandma? What have they done with her? My little mind and my imagination combined could not put any reason to what I was observing versus what I had been told. I was lost in my darkness of confusion.

How do you explain to a young boy that Grandma was in heaven, while her body was in the ground? If Grandma was in the ground right here in front of me, then how can you say she is in heaven? My mind spiraled.

Quietly the voice that had so many times brought peace and assurance to a troubled little boy, said, "Let's go for a walk," as he placed that strong arm around my shoulder. "There's a place down by the lake. You wait here and I'll be right back."

With that he left the dock and started slowly walking around the edge of the lake, stopping every few seconds, bending over and picking up something. His actions made even my imagination go off the charts! Paw-Paw is a smart man, but what is he up to? I've done some wild things in my life . . . but nothing like what's he doing now!

Returning to the dock, "Move over, Son," Paw-Paw said as he sat back down. I knew the expression on my face, "What is he up to?" was speaking volumes. Slowly Paw-Paw laid out the treasures between us that he had picked up, making sure they were in a certain order.

"Notice the order, and especially the color," he said as he meticulously placed them side by side.

There was first a yellow-golden flower, followed by an ugly black stone. Looking up at me, he said, "But there is hope!"

"Hope? I don't follow," I questioned.

"You will in a moment," he explained as he placed the rock back down. Next came a bright red wild strawberry, which he set ever so gently between the ugly black stone and the all-white chicken feather, "and we must not forget the green grass," which was last. The chicken feather hadn't confused my thinking as I knew that the old mother hen would often hide her eggs down by the pond's edge in hopes no one would find them. That was some kind of' hope, so maybe this was going someplace.

Looking down at the items lined up I knew it had to be some mystical ancient Indian ceremonial rite Paw-Paw was about to share with me.

Once again I began thinking about that "show and tell" assignment for the first day of school.

Would I share this ancient Indian ceremonial rite, or crossing the Mason Dixie Border? Of course, if I chose the latter, I would have to make up stuff that I missed while asleep in the back seat of the car when crossing the border, but I was good at that, so that wouldn't be any problem. Maybe I could tie the two together?

Smiling a smile that I had seen before, Paw-Paw was letting me know that what he was about to say was "law and gospel," wrapped in love. Knowing that look made me realize that I had nothing to fear; that I could relax and just listen.

"First of all, Grandma didn't do anything wrong, it was just her time to die. She didn't die to make us sad; she loved us too much for that. Her heart just gave out, and that is why she died.

You, see, we all must die at some time or another. But the real question shouldn't be, "Why did we die," but "Where do we go after we die?" That is a choice we have to make now, not after we die.

"Let me tell you a story*, using all these things you saw me collecting a few minutes ago, "Paw- Paw continued as I looked on, curiosity about to "kill" me.

"Look at this lovely yellow flower, perfect in a way only God could make it. It reminds me of a beautiful place where there is a street made out of gold. No more perfect place was ever created. It's Heaven, of course. There is no pain, no sickness, no death, no crying - perfect. The best part is that Jesus is there! But there is one thing that isn't in Heaven, sin."

Slowly he picked up the black rock as if he were uncomfortable even talking about it. "This black rock reminds us of the darkness of sin. It's the bad things people do. It's as if we can't see God in the right way because sin has blinded us. I know you know what sin is since we have talked before about lying and disobedience. But sin is anything we do or think that would be against God's laws.

---

* Idea from Child Evangelism Fellowship

And the Bible says that all of us have sinned—Grandma, and yes, your Paw-Paw too. You may be thinking that if there is no sin in Heaven, but that all have done sins, how is anyone going to get to live in that wonderful place?"

I was indeed thinking that very thing since everyone had said that Grandma was in Heaven and Paw-Paw had just said Grandma had sinned. I was more than ready for the next part of this story!

"O, yes, the red is for the blood of Jesus," he said, as he picked up the strawberry and sadly shook his head. "Notice the color, Son, because this is the best reminder of all. God loved us SO much that He sent His Son, Jesus, to live on this earth. You know we celebrate Christmas because Jesus was born as a baby. He grew up, never having one sin of His own, and at age 33

He allowed Himself to be nailed to a cross to take the punishment for our sins."

Picking up two sticks, he made a small cross. "And what came out of his hands and feet where the nails were pounded in? Yes, blood. The Bible says that the blood of Jesus washes away ALL of the bad things we have done - ALL our sins - the lying, disobedience, stealing, disrespect, hating - ALL."

"But Jesus didn't stay dead! He came back alive again—something only God could do! This feather is white, like something very clean. We need to be "cleaned up" and have those sins taken away. When we ask Jesus to come into our life, He comes in and washes away our sins, something like a chalkboard that has all the writing erased. He "erases" our sins!" But He doesn't come into a person's life uninvited. Every person must choose to say, 'Please come in and forgive my sins.'"

"Have you asked Jesus to forgive your sins, Paw-Paw? Will you see Grandma again?"

"I sure did, years ago! And although I am sad that she has died, I know I'll see her again."

By this time, listening to Paw Paw and remembering what I had been taught in Sunday school, it was becoming clearer than ever before, that our sin was a really bad thing, and I wanted my sins forgiven so I could be sure I would be in Heaven with Jesus someday and that I would see Grandma again, too! I wanted to choose Jesus so I could be in Heaven and not hell when it was my time to die.

"Paw-Paw, don't forget the green grass!" He smiled as he picked up the handful of grass. "O, I won't. It's very important. The green grass stands for growing. When we invite Him into our lives, we become His child and He wants us to grow to know Him better and to become more like Him each day. Reading the Bible, praying, going to church - those things help us to know Him better and then He helps us to do what is right. The Bible says, "The Lord is my helper..."

The greatest choice we will ever make is choosing life, everlasting life that only comes from trusting in Jesus for the forgiveness of sins.

And so it is...